To Mary,

CROSSROADS
A Camino tale

May the sun always shine and the world be at your Back

F. R. MERRILL

JJ Merrill

DISCLAIMER:

I walked *The Camino del Norte* in 2006. From that experience I have referenced towns, terrain, and landmarks. However, incidents, the story relayed, and all characters in this book are fictitious.

For more information on the *Camino del Norte*:

To view the largest incense burner (*Botafumerio*) in action in the Cathedral de Santiago go to: <u>Botafumeiro a Santiago Compostela YouTube.</u>

For more on the ***Camino Del Norte***, maps, photos, and distances, go to: www.santiago-compostela.net

Photos:

Were used with permission of the photographer F.R. Merrill from the family's archive, and are from the collection of F.R. Merrill.

Map created by F.R. Merrill

Cover design by Frances Rinaldi and Tal Thompson

*This book is dedicated to
those who believe in miracles and to
those who have walked the path of St. James.*

CONTENT

ACKNOWLEDGEMENTS:

I have been blessed to be part of a wonderful editing group. My sincere thanks to Pat McDonough for allowing me to become a member of this amazing group. I am also grateful to Linda Jump, Ed von Koenigseck, and Andy Vazquez for editing my novel, and ever so much more. I am grateful for their never-ending encouragement and friendship.

Thanks to Mary Volberding for her continued support and editing review. A special thanks to my longtime friend, Angela Lockhart for taking a chance and hiking Spain with me. Thanks to Sue Rapp for keeping such a great blog of the trip, being a great friend, and wonderful traveling companion. Thanks to Jan Drever for plotting ways for adventure.

As always, my unending gratitude to my daughters Angela and Marie, my grandson Bradley, and my husband Andre who continue to support me through the challenges that accompany writing a novel.

I'd like to thank Dr. Wayne Dyer for writing *There Is A Spiritual Answer to Every Question*. I repeatedly read excerpts from his book while walking *The Camino*. The book's messages comforted me then, and still do.

Past miracles are often revealed as legend, and legends are what present miracles are made of.

F.R. Merrill

ST. FRANCIS PRAYER
OF PEACE

Lord make me an instrument of your peace
Where there is hatred, Let me sow love;
Where there is injury, pardon;
Where there is doubt, faith;
Where there is despair, hope;
Where there is darkness, light;
And where there is sadness, Joy.
O Divine Master grant that I may
Not so much seek to be consoled
As to console; To be understood,
As to understand; To be loved as to love.
For it is in giving that we receive,
It is in pardoning that we are pardoned.
And it is in dying that we are born to eternal life.
Amen

CAMINO DEL NORTE - 550 miles

PHASE 1 Hondarribia to Santander Estmated 321 Kilo./200 miles

1. Honarribia to San Sebastian
2. San Sebastian to Zarautz
3. Zarautz to Deba
4. Deba to Markina- Xemein
5. Markina-Xemein to Gernika
6. Gernika to Lezama
7. Lezama to Bilbao
8. Bilbao to Portugalete
9. Portugalete to Castro Urdiales
10. Castro Urdiales to Laredo
11. Laredo to Noja
12. Noja to Santander

PHASE 2 Santander to Oviedo Estimated 241 kilo./150 miles

13. Santander to Santillana del Mar
14. Santillana del Mar to Comillas
15. Comillas to Unguera
16. Unguera to Llanes
17. Llanes to Ribadesella
18. Ribadesella to Colunga
19. Colunga to Villaviciosa
20. Villaviciosa to Oviedo

PHASE 3 Oviedo to Santiago Estimated 402 kilo./250 miles

21. Oviedo to Aviles
22. Aviles to Cudillero
23. Cudillero to Cadavedo
24. Cadavedo to Luarca
25. Luarca to LaCaridad

26. LaCaridad to Ribadeo
27. Ribadeo to Lourenza
28. Lourenza to Abadin
29. Abadin to Vilalba
30. Villaba to Baamonde
31. Baamonde to Sobrado
    dos Monxes
32. Sobrado dos Monxes to Arzua

☆ 33. Arzua to Santiago de Compostela

MAP OF SPAIN

Numbers represent stops along the way.

1

1992 – DOWNSTATE CORRECTIONAL FACILITY, FISHKILL, N.Y.

Dressed in a floral-print spaghetti-strapped dress, Honey approached the entrance to the correctional facility. The prison guard watched her hips sway gracefully side to side as he greeted her with his usual flirtatious smile and pushed the button to unlock the heavy restraining door.

Her blond hair rested on her bare shoulders and high heels clicked rhythmically on the gray concrete floor as she passed into the lifeless hallway and walked to the next door.

Although attractive, unpleasant events in Honey's youth led her to live reclusively. Early on she discovered she had a gift for mathematics. Working as an accountant offered the solitude she desired. Only one person had been able to break through the barriers she had self induced over the years, Dr. Ivan Harris. She waited patiently for the door-lock to release.

Once she was inside the room, a guard directed Honey to a chair at a long counter in front of a small glass window. There she waited for the man she loved, Dr. Ivan Harris.

When Ivan took his seat on the opposite side of the window, she frowned. "Ivan, you're looking thinner than the last time I was here. Are you feeling okay? Is there anything I can get for you?"

"No. I'm fine, Honey. Thanks for putting funds into my account. Were you able to get the information I asked for?"

"Somewhat. Amanda has gone home to Fishkill, N.Y to visit her mother whose tour is on break for a couple of months. I connected with a friend of Faith's who has been keeping me up on their movements."

Ivan's jaw tightened. His voice was cold, "I've waited too long already. Take whatever money you need from my account. Go to Fishkill. Do what you have to."

"Ivan, I've worked my way into a circle of Faith's friends. I'll know more in a couple of days."

Ivan's tone remained harsh. "I want Faith to suffer. I've already waited too long."

He leaned in close to the window and whispered. "I want her daughter taken care of. I thought I could trust you."

Honey felt a pang in her chest. Hurt by his remark, she managed to remain controlled as she answered, "You can. After all you've done for me you know you can trust me. I just need a little more information before I can put your plan into action. I need to find out if her daughter is going back to school, or staying home for the summer. I'll have answers next week for sure."

"See that you do."

When Honey left the prison she drove home frustrated over Ivan's reaction to her progress. She understood his disappointment. Faith Straton had killed her husband and while Ivan was unconscious she had placed a gun in his hand to frame him for murder. Still, Honey had done everything Ivan had asked. She was even going to commit murder for him. Upset over his questioning her loyalty she took a moment to regain her composure. She felt her shoulders relax as she remembered how much he had helped her over they years. She owed him her life. Without his help she would be in a mental institution.

After four months on tour, Faith Straton was going home.

She drove with the windows down. The wind blew her straight black hair in all directions. Happy to be heading home, along with the voice on the radio she sang loudly, *I Love Rock and Roll.*

Fresh clean air and crisp lingering smells of cut grass and flowering bushes permeated the inside of her aging Volvo station-wagon, *What a great day to listen to the Joan Jett and the Blackhearts.*

When Faith pulled into her driveway she noticed the white paint on the picket fence surrounding the front yard had faded. She entered her suburban home and was pleased to find the lights on.

She found fresh flowers had been placed in a vase on the dining-room table, and she knew Tom, her fiancée with the help of her friend Tina Strouse were responsible. She smiled. *What a nice surprise.*

She opened the dining-room drapes. Through the sliding glass doors she saw a backyard of un-pruned trees and bushes, an overgrown neglected vegetable bed, and rusty lawn furniture. She sighed. *It has been awhile since I've been home.*

Her thoughts shifted to her daughter Amanda who was coming home on break from college. Faith's divorce had put a strain on the mother-daughter relationship. After the murder of Amanda's father, Carl, two years before, tensions between them intensified. Amanda's complicated bereavement slowed the healing process. It took months before the two were able to communicate without antagonism. It was going to be good to see Amanda. Between her touring and Amanda's college schedule, it had been months since they'd been able to get together.

Grateful for Tom's and Tina's attempts to put her house in order, Faith stared out the window. There was still a lot that needed to be done around the house, but first she needed to make a stop at the dance studio.

At 11a.m., Faith went into her studio. Tina, punctual as always, stood behind the counter.

She noticed that Tina had cut her brown wavy hair. Short tight curls embraced her soft-featured face. Tina had lost the girlish figure of a dancer due to the stress of caring for her ailing husband. She looked as if she'd added 50 pounds.

The added weight, fatigue lines and puffiness under her eyes would have scared Faith, if these weary signs weren't quickly offset by the sweet sparkle in Tina's eyes and her genuinely warm smile.

Faith walked across the large room. The slight bounce of oak flooring under her feet brought back happy memories of young dancers in front of shining mirrors, or twirling on tiptoe across the studio floor.

Tina stepped out from behind the counter and gave Faith a big hug. "I can't believe you're home. It's been so long."

After Tina released Faith from her grip, she pulled two chairs close together. Once seated, Faith said, "Tina, the studio looks better than when I left. It feels strange to be home after such a long absence. I wish you had taken my offer to become my partner. I don't know what I'm going to do without you."

Tina leaned forward. "Faith, you know I've enjoyed every minute here managing the studio, but I never wanted ownership responsibility. Now more than ever, I'm grateful I didn't make that move. Jimmy is getting worse."

Faith listened intently as Tina described her husband, Jimmy's condition.

"I thought I would be able to stay for at least another year, but it's clear I can't. Kim, the gal we hired last year is doing a great job. If she runs into trouble she can reach me by phone anytime, or come by the house."

"Tina, you must think I'm selfish, worrying about the studio when you are going through so much. I'm not sure what I can do, but I'm here for you." Faith said.

Tina scooted back in her chair. "You may regret what you just said. I do have a favor to ask. Lea has offered to take time off from her college schedule to watch her father so I can go on a pilgrimage. If I don't get away soon, it will be a long time before I'll be able to get away again. Kim is also experienced enough to manage the dance studio." Tina smiled sheepishly as her eyes twinkled. "I bet you're wondering, so what does that have to do with me?"

"A little."

"Faith, you're home for a few months, and since business at the studio slows down during the summer, I was thinking you could come with me."

"Wow, what kind of pilgrimage?"

"The one your friend, Jocelyn, is going on. She called to get your Fishkill address so she could mail you the information. We talked for some time and I asked if she'd mind if I came along. She said that it would be fine. The more the merrier."

Faith had met Jocelyn while training for a marathon while working on her off-Broadway show *Blackbird Hear My Words*. While the show toured around the U.S., whenever Faith was in Manhattan she and Jocelyn went for a run. Hearing Tina's plea, Faith couldn't help but think that if Jocelyn was looking at this pilgrimage, it was for personal development. She wasn't into spiritual quests. What she enjoyed was a good physical challenge.

Faith smiled. "Well, Tina, you've got my attention. Tell me more."

Tina sat straight in her chair. Energy poured out of every cell. "It's called *The Camino*. It's a 550-mile hike in Spain following the path of Saint James. Jocelyn did a different route last year called *The French Route*. Now she's ready to hike *The Northern Route*. Jocelyn said it will be tougher, but prettier. If we go all the way to *The End of the World, Cape Finisterre*, and stay for the Festival of St. James, we'll be in Spain six weeks. I've started going to the gym and walking to get ready." Tina's eyes beamed with delight. "I know it will be tough, but with your help I know I can do it."

A hundred questions churned in Faith's head. Could she be out of communication for six weeks? Was Tina strong enough to make this trip? Other thoughts surfaced. She was finally going to have time to spend with Tom and Amanda, did she want to take off now?

By the look on Faith's face, Tina could see she was giving the idea some thought.

Faith looked at Tina. "I'm not going to make any promises. I need to think about it more. What do you know about the trip?"

Tina picked up a stack of brochures. "Jocelyn mailed these to me. I also went to the library and did some research. It sounds wonderful. In the 9th century, the tomb of the Apostle Saint James was discovered in Spain.

Legend has it he had traveled from Jerusalem to Spain carrying the word of peace. Upon his death, his remains were brought to and buried in the city, now known as Santiago. A small chapel was built in his honor where today stands the great Cathedral De Santiago. It has been said that even after he was beheaded, he appeared during horrible battles. Seeing the apparition, soldiers on both sides put down their weapons and followed him in peace. Sightings were made long after the Crusades." Tina took a breath and continued to read from the brochure. "On July 25, 1483 St. James appeared on yet another battlefield, weapons were dropped and the Central African Kingdom of the Congo was saved. Thus began the Festival of St. James. Since the discovery of the tomb of St. James, hundreds of pilgrims have made the pilgrimage to Santiago."

Faith laughed, teasing. "You're excited about this trip aren't you? I can't believe so many people have hiked this pilgrimage for so long and I never heard of it before. Do you have the dates of the trip?"

"Jocelyn said they plan to start the first week in June. That's less than a month away. The terrain looks mountainous and runs mostly along the northern coast of Spain. I know we will have to hustle to be ready."

"I'll tell you what. I'll call Jocelyn to see who else is coming. I'll get more details and figure out the cost. I also need to talk it over with Tom and check my funds. Six weeks in Spain may be over my budget."

Tina's shoulders relaxed. "Bet you weren't expecting all this, were you?

"I have to admit, you've caught me off guard."

Driving home, Faith considered how much she owed Tina. She wouldn't have survived the last two years without her help running her dance studio. But, she also owed Tom and Amanda for their patience and support. Attempting to come up with a plan that would make everyone happy, she wondered if Amanda would like to hike Spain, and how Tom would feel about meeting her in Spain at the end of the trip.

Happy to make it home before Amanda's arrival, Faith prepared dinner. While cutting onions, she decided to call Jocelyn for more information before mentioning anything to Tom and Amanda.

Faith dialed Jocelyn's number.

"Hello." Jocelyn answered.

"Hi. This is Faith."

With a chuckle in her voice, Jocelyn said, "Guess you talked to your friend Tina today. She is very excited about hiking the *Camino*. I know she wants you to do it too. Did she talk you into it?"

"It sounds interesting, but I have a few questions. Do you have time to talk?

Without hesitation, Jocelyn replied, "I've got time. Shoot."

"Who else is going?"

"So far, Ada, the gal we trained with for the last marathon and an acquaintance, Honey. I don't think you've met her. Ada has volunteered to room with her. You know me. I like having my own space."

Faith hesitated, uncomfortable in asking. "How do you think the girls would feel about having Amanda join us?"

"I'll mention it, but I'm sure they won't care. The problem will be whether your group will be able to find accommodations. We've already booked. It may be difficult for you to find places nearby still available."

With a soft chuckle, Faith said. "My bet is Tina has already started looking."

"My guess is you're right. I'll call after I talk to the gals." "Great."

Before hanging up the phone, Faith asked, "Jocelyn, this hike doesn't sound like a trip for amateurs. I'm sure Tina will find this trip physically challenging. We might have to go slower than the rest of the group. Will that be a problem?"

"Not for me. We will all travel at our own pace. The good news is that if you two don't show in the evening, someone will know to go looking for you."

While Faith listened to Jocelyn she considered the challenge involved in walking slowly with Tina and determined it shouldn't be too difficult.

Faith still had concerns. "Jocelyn, can you give me a rough idea of how much the trip will cost?"

"Not including the airfare, I think it came to about $2,800 per person. The exchange rate is not in our favor, but it's not too bad."

"It sounds like you planned this trip very cost effectively, but I've still got some head scratching to do before I can make a definite decision. I'll let you know if I can make it."

"Great. If you come into town, call me. We can go for a run and catch up."

"Sounds good. I'll talk to you soon."

Faith hung up the phone and went to the kitchen. She cut carrots and celery into thin strips, made a vegetable dip, and prepared chicken salad sandwiches.

When Faith was done with food preparations, she put on her yard gloves and went to the backyard to pull weeds. For the first time in two years, she felt domestic. While weeding, the thought of hiking Spain with Amanda grew on her. Although, knowing her daughter, she figured she'd probably enjoy the trip better if one of Amanda's friends joined them. It would be a financial stretch, but the more she thought about it, the more convinced she became that it would be worth every penny.

After an hour of pulling out entangled weeds that were choking her azaleas, beads of perspiration rolled down the side of Faith's face.

Lost in thought, she didn't hear Amanda open the sliding door. "Mom, how long do you plan on staying out there?"

Faith took off her gloves and went to Amanda. "Hi sweetheart, how was the drive? Hope you're hungry."

"The drive was okay. I took my time and stopped along the way. As for eating, you know I'm always ready for that."

"Glad to have you home. I'll clean up and meet you in the kitchen."

Amanda gave her mother a gentle hug. Faith squeezed her tightly.

After Faith showered and Amanda settled in, they met in the kitchen. "I was thinking about going with Tina to Spain."

"What's the occasion?" Amanda asked.

"It's a hike across the Northern part of Spain."

"Sounds like fun. How long will you be gone?" Amanda asked.

"Six weeks."

Faith pleased to see her daughter's interest continued, "I'll let you know how things progress. Feel like heading into town and doing a little shopping?"

"Since when do you like shopping?"

"I'm still not a big fan of shopping, but I figured you'd rather shop than pull weeds on your first day home."

"To tell the truth Mom, weeding doesn't sound good to me at any time, but I came knowing there would be work to be done." After a short pause, Amanda asked, "Do you think Rachael can come shopping with us? I haven't seen her in months."

"Sure."

Amanda phoned Rachael. With the phone in her hand, Amanda called out, "Mom, Rachael can go. When should I tell her to be ready?"

"We can be at her house in 20 minutes. Will that give her enough time to get ready?"

"She said that's fine."

When Faith and Amanda arrived at Rachael's they found her waiting outside on her front porch.

Rachael got in Faith's car and within minutes they were parked and shopping in Fishkill's Mall.

"Shopping in Fishkill is sure different than in Manhattan," Amanda said.

"Sure is. Are you taking summer classes or taking off for summer break?" Rachael asked.

"I haven't made up my mind, yet." Amanda answered.

Enjoying the girls company, Faith thought. *Rachael is such a great kid, maybe she'll be able to come along. She is well traveled and speaks Spanish.*

After several hours spent enjoying shopping with the girls, Faith dropped off Rachael, and she and Amanda headed home. Rounding the corner, Faith noticed the 1983 classic, white-with-red-topped, Cadillac convertible in her driveway. *Tom drove here in his Aunt Laura's car instead of renting a car.*

Inside, Faith and Amanda placed packages on the large oak dining table, and found Tom under the kitchen sink with a wrench in hand.

"Tom, what's wrong with the sink?"

Tom pulled his head out from under the sink. "When I came into the kitchen there was water on the floor. I discovered the leak was coming from under the sink. Probably didn't show up until now since no one had used the sink for awhile." Tom looked at the packages they had set on the table. "Looks like you two had a good day."

"Yeah, looks like our day was much better than yours," Amanda said. "Mom, if you don't need me, I'm going to take my stuff to my room."

"That's fine. I'll call when supper is ready."

As soon as Amanda left the room, Tom, holding his sweaty body away from Faith, leaned in and kissed her tenderly on the cheek.

"Tom, you just got here and already you're fixing things. Sit down and rest. Want something to drink?"

"Sure. I saw you had some lemonade."

Tom sat down at the kitchen table and stared hard at Faith. "Okay, what are you up to?"

"You know me too well."

Faith pulled a chair next to Tom. After she shared Tina's plight, what she knew about the *Camino*, and her feelings about taking Amanda on the pilgrimage, she waited for Tom's response.

"Faith, I can work my vacation around the trip. I could meet you at the end of the trip. After the gals head for home, we could spend some time exploring together. I've never been to Spain, and what a great experience for Amanda."

Faith jumped up from her chair, flung her arms around his neck and kissed him passionately. "You're the best."

2

CHANGE OF PLAN

Two weeks after her last visit with Ivan, Honey sat anxiously awaiting his entrance into the prison's waiting area. She knew he wouldn't be happy with her making another change in the plan.

When she saw Ivan, her chest tightened. Before he sat down, she said, "Both Faith and Amanda have decided to go to Spain for six weeks."

She waited for him to sit and respond. She had learned to be patient. He had been her psychiatrist for 11 years. His mildly unkempt blond wavy hair, his lean body build and pleasant demeanor were the things that made her fall for him instantly. He had always been empathetic to her needs. They had reviewed years of abuse by her father and then her husband. During the time Dr. Harris treated her, she kept her feelings for him a secret, knowing he would never entertain a relationship with a patient.

Following his incarceration, she wrote Dr. Harris and came to his aid.

After two months of visiting him in prison, she professed her feelings of love and her belief in his innocence.

To her wonderment, he accepted her announcement with approval. Over time, she became his confidant, and ultimately was to become his avenger. But at this moment, he looked entirely unsatisfied.

The words raced out of her mouth. "I thought Amanda was going to stay in school for the summer session. She's decided to take off for summer break and go to Spain. Anyway, I'm sure I can still make things work out to your satisfaction."

Deep lines furrowed between his brow and his mouth pursed. He scolded her in a brittle voice. "I'm losing confidence in your ability to take care of this matter."

With a forced smile, Honey said, "Faith's friend, Jocelyn, told me a group of women are planning to go to Spain. Faith is bringing Amanda and one of Amanda's friends with her. If I go with them, I can complete the task in Spain. It will be easier for me to get close to Amanda without suspicion. The setting will be perfect for an accidental death."

Honey noticed the tension on Ivan's face relax slightly. "When will this trip take place?"

"This month I already put down a deposit so I can go with them, hoping you'd find the plan workable."

"I still have some hiking equipment including backpacks and poles in storage. Check them out before purchasing new equipment. And this time, make it work."

Speaking clearly and softly, Honey cautiously relayed more details of the trip. Then, she waited for his response.

Ivan nodded in a reserved but positive manner. "Write this address down. I'll get a message to him that you will be coming. He will have the added necessary tools you will need to complete your mission."

Before she stood to leave, she said, "I'm meeting Jocelyn to go for a short run in Central Park. I'll have more information on Faith and Amanda afterward. I promise you won't be disappointed."

3

PREPARATIONS

The sun's rays worked their way under the turquoise curtains in Faith's bedroom. Her eyes opened. She looked at the clock on the end table. She knew she better get moving. Tina would arrive at 7:00 a.m. sharp. She was never late. And after weeks of walking, going to the gym, and having lost five pounds, she'd be ready to tackle a six-mile walk.

Faith made her bed and then pulled out and placed her new hiking clothes, shoes, poles and backpack on it. The hiking attire was foreign to her usual running clothes. Hiking boots were heavy compared to the lightness of tennis shoes. When she ran she felt free of the restraints that poles and the weight of a backpack produced.

She showered, but before she had dried off, Tina was knocking at her front door. Faith tossed on a robe, went to, and opened the door.

"Good morning, sleepyhead," Tina said.

"I'm almost ready. But I need my coffee before we go. This is a dry run. I see no reason to start suffering before the pilgrimage."

"You know we'll start earlier than this in Spain."

"I know. I still don't see the need to start suffering."

"Get ready, I'll fix coffee. Does Amanda drink coffee?"

"She does, but she spent the night at Rachael's. They're going to do some last minute shopping for the trip today. She'll be home this evening. I think Rachael needed heavier socks and Amanda needed some small items. They plan to fly into Paris first to spend a couple of days there. It's a place they've both always wanted to visit."

While Tina made toast and poached a couple of eggs, Faith got dressed. After breakfast, they drove to a park outside the city limits. They had stuffed their backpacks with towels for bulk and a ten-pound weight to imitate the allotted 25 pounds. For a more perfect simulation, they filled the soft rubber water holders inside their backpacks with water. They adjusted the flexible rubber tubes of their camelbacks so they could take a drink without having to take their hands off their hiking poles. With hiking poles in hand, they went up the well-worn trail. The dirt was smooth, and to Faith the grade of incline made for an easy climb. The air was fresh and cool in the shade.

Faith normally walked this six-mile route at a leisurely pace, taking an hour and half, but not today. As soon as they came to a slight incline, Tina's breathing became forced, and she had to stop and wait several minutes to catch her breath. At the end of their first mile which took 30 minutes, Faith's concerns over the trip escalated. She calculated, *13 to 20 miles a day. At this pace it's going to take us 6 ½ to 10 hours without even stopping to eat. And that's if she doesn't go slower the farther we go.*

By the third mile, Faith's concerns increased as Tina's pace decreased. Faith offered recommendations. "Breathe deeper, lift your knees and take higher steps." With each step Faith took she felt as if a log, tied to her ankles, was burrowing deep into the ground holding her back.

One of Faith's shoelaces was untied. Instead of bending at her knees, she leaned over from her waist, and the weight in her backpack rolled toward her head causing her to lose her balance. She fell sideways onto the ground.

Tina struggled to get to her side. "Are you okay?"

Laughing, she answered. "I'm fine." While thinking, *This is my punishment for being impatient with Tina.*

After her mishap, whenever Faith found herself waiting for Tina, she meditated. Prayers and meditation helped to calm her. Still, by the end of the seven miles, seven hours later, it took all of Faith's strength to give Tina words of praise and encouragement.

That night, the results of their first training attempt turned into nightmares for Faith. In her dream, a giant, green spider, larger than a person climbed onto her bedspread. Its open mouth revealed a bright red tongue. She screamed and sat awake in bed.

Unable to shake the nightmare from her thoughts, she went to the kitchen to get a glass of water. While drinking the water, she heard footsteps approaching the kitchen. She turned and found Amanda standing in the doorway.

"Mom, I thought I heard someone scream. Did you hear it?"

"I screamed. I had a strange nightmare, but I'm fine. How was your day?"

"Good. I think Rachael has everything she needs, and I'm all set, too. So, how is your training with Tina going?"

"Pretty well. She's making good progress." It was a small white lie, but she didn't want to let Amanda or the others know her concerns. She didn't want to create any doubts about Tina's ability to walk.

"Then, what's up with the nightmare? Are you worried that the house renovations won't be finished before you leave for Spain?"

"Maybe, but Tom is coming in a few days and I'm sure we'll get things back in order before we leave. Then again, I don't want Tom to feel pressured. He doesn't get much time off from work. Anyway, I'm fine. Probably just something I ate. How about you? Getting excited about the trip?"

"I am. We were thinking about bringing regular clothes to Paris and then shipping them home."

"Sounds like a great idea. Sorry I woke you. Hope you can get back to sleep."

"Mom, you know sleeping has never been a problem for me."

With a soft giggle, Faith replied, "I know.

In her bedroom, to help keep the awful vision from returning, Faith directed her thoughts to prayer. The words were adapted from the thoughts and prayers from three of her mentors: Chief Joseph, Paramahansa Yogananda, and Ma Yogashakti Saraswati. These words never failed her.

> A hundred thousand years have passed; yet, I hear the distant beat of my father's drum.
>
> I hear the drums throughout the land. I feel the beat within my heart.
>
> In this land of beauty, I sit in peace,
>
> And offer up to you flowers filled with the essence of desire-less-ness.
>
> Let my ears hear only truthful and honorable words.
>
> Let my lips speak only truthful and honorable words.
>
> Let my eyes see only truthful and honorable things.

May I never leave God and may God never leave me.

The drums shall beat, so my heart shall beat, and I shall live a hundred thousand years.

In the presence of a few minutes, sleep came sweetly.

Over the next few days while Faith and Tina walked to test their equipment, Faith found her shoes didn't fit properly. Blisters formed on her little toes. With time running out, she bought a new pair of hiking boots with hopes she could break them in before the trip.

Tina decided to spend more time getting ready for the hike by walking on a treadmill at the gym so she could spend time with Jimmy before their departure.

Tom kept Faith busy making mild improvements to the house and yard, and never let a day go by without the two taking a long jaunt together.

One night, lying next to Tom in bed, snuggled up safe in his arms, Faith questioned her sanity about going on the pilgrimage.

As if Tom could hear her thoughts, he pulled her close and said, "You're going to have a great time. Things are going to work out with Tina."

"Thanks. I love you."

Tom kissed her gently. "That goes double for me."

4

THE SECRET

Honey wore a disguise, a brown wig and a wide-brimmed hat adorned her head. Over a non-descript dress she wore a long black trench coat. A yellow and black plaid scarf draped her neck, rested over her chin, and hung over her shoulders.

She stood for a moment teetering on two unsteady legs. Her eyes focused on the dilapidated three-story building in front of her. As instructed, she had taken a cab. She was surprised Ivan had sent her into such a dangerous section in the Bronx.

She came to and stared at the front door of the address Ivan had given her. After she knocked, she sensed the presence of someone on the other side of the door looking at her through the peep-hole. Her muscles tightened.

A clanking chain hit the door which gave way to the door opening. An elderly, gray-haired man dressed in worn clothes, smelling of cigar, gestured for her to enter.

The main room was untidy. On the coffee table, between the couch and the TV, there were days-old Chinese food containers and pizza boxes. She glanced into the kitchen. She saw unwashed dishes that looked as if they had been there for months.

She began to introduce herself, but the man didn't give her a chance to continue. "Names aren't important. The less we know about each other, the better. A mutual friend told me to gather a few supplies for you. This package will travel well in your suitcase."

He led her to a desk in the room. It looked out of place, all neat and clean. Here he kept his tools of destruction purposefully and carefully arranged. He pointed to a needle and syringe, "This poison kills within seconds. Little trace remains in the system after only two hours."

He took a wooden back-scratching device, popped off an end, wrapped the needle and syringe in plastic, and gently inserted them into the tube.

"It should be safe inside this wooden case until you are ready to use it," he said.

Honey pulled out her wallet to pay him.

The man's gaze was detached as he spoke, "It's been taken care of. I'll call a cab and ask the driver to meet you two blocks south of here."

Anxiously, she made her way to the cab.

Not until Honey stood safe and secure in her city apartment did she feel her shoulders relax. She pulled the backscratcher out of her bag, and placed it next to her backpack. She hoped it would make it through customs as planned.

5

ANTICIPATION

Excited about the trip, but anxious about leaving Tom and her home for six weeks, Faith snuggled close to Tom, procrastinating from getting out of bed.

He put his arm around her waist and pulled her close. "I'll miss you, too. Just remember you can always fly home, or I can fly to you."

It was as if he had read her thoughts. Faith rolled over to face him. With eyes now wide open, she softly said, "I love you."

After a few minutes of blissful cuddling, Faith looked at Tom. His eyes were closed. She felt blessed he had come back into her life. He'd been her rock through the last few years.

They met in the Catskills at the Woodstock festival in 1969. Tom was in his senior high school year, and Faith was in her junior year. Tom was Faith's first true love. At 16 years of age, she had been devastated by the breakup. Twenty years later they reconnected, and their childhood romance blossomed.

Sitting up in bed she made a quick check of the bags propped along the wall. She had packed and unpacked the bag so many times, picking and choosing what 25 pounds would be essential and what could be left behind. Still, she feared she had forgotten something important.

Tom sat up. "Stop worrying. Smoke is coming off the top of your head. I'll fix coffee while you get dressed."

Out of the shower, Faith dressed in clothes she had purchased at a thrift store. She and Tina bought clothes they would wear the first couple of days in Spain, and then would give away to reduce the weight in their packs.

When Faith entered the kitchen, Tom greeted her with a warm, "Good morning, Sunshine." He handed her a cup of coffee.

"Thanks." Her face softened and a gentle, sweet smile surfaced. "I'm going to miss you."

"Once you're on that plane and with your friends, you're going to forget all about me."

"That's not going to happen."

After Tom went to get dressed and she finished her coffee, Faith pulled the duffle bag, hiking poles and backpack to the front door.

Tom finished getting dressed and headed for the kitchen before he noticed Faith's bag was missing from the bedroom. "Faith, where's your bag?"

"It's by the front door." She was now sitting at the kitchen table. He leaned down and kissed her gently on the back of her neck.

Following a leisurely breakfast, Faith went through her checklist once again. Accommodatingly Tom said, "Check," and "check" again and again. Then, he laughed out loud. "How many times do we need to check this 25-pound bag for three sets of clothes and your toothbrush? We don't have to pick up Tina until later this afternoon. You could wear your clothes out if you keep going through that bag."

"Okay, so I'm a little nervous."

"It's not like you haven't traveled overseas before. Why are you so anxious about this trip?"

"Other trips I've been on were tours, or I was visiting friends. I've never hiked in another country before. I'm also concerned about Tina and Amanda."

"I've got an idea. Let's go out for lunch. On the way home, we'll stop, get a bottle of champagne and enjoy a glass outside in your newly weeded yard."

After lunch, Tom and Faith enjoyed their drinks on the back porch. Faith lay back in a chaise lounge and fell asleep.

After an hour, Faith awoke to find Tom reading a book quietly by her side. "Tom, what time is it?"

"You only dozed off for an hour. It's still early. Want to go for a walk?"

"No, I think I'll just stay here, close my eyes, and meditate. Maybe that will calm my nerves."

Faith struggled through the next couple of hours, and was relieved when Tom came back and asked, "Are you ready? I think we should get going. Tina should be ready."

"I guess so."

While Tom carried her bag to the car, Faith locked the front door, and thought, *I'm really going on a pilgrimage in Spain.*

When they pulled up to Tina's house, her bag was sitting outside the front door.

When Tina opened the door, Faith could see Lea, Tina's daughter, sitting beside her father, Jim. Tina kissed Jim good-bye. Lea leaped up to hug her mother. "Have fun, Mom."

"I will. And you two better behave while I'm gone."

Tom lifted Tina's duffle bag which held her backpack and poles, and looked back over his shoulder. "Jim, I'll call you later, after I get the dancing girls lined up."

Jim smiled and, as best he could muster replied, "Good deal."

From the moment Tina left her house she began to review flight schedules, as well as the hotel arrangements for the next few days.

The drive from Fishkill to the Newark airport flew by. By leaving at 4:00 p.m. the evening traffic rush was just starting to build. Faith was pleased when they arrived with time to spare.

Tom parked and helped carry their bags to check-in. "After you two check your bags, let's get something to eat." Tina was so nervous that without even asking to see what Faith might like to do, she refused. Faith shrugged her shoulders, and Tom gave Faith a loving glance.

Once their bags were checked, and tickets were in hand, Faith and Tina turned to Tom and waved their last good-bye before heading to go through security.

Faith felt a flutter in her chest and a slight tremor in her legs. Sitting and waiting for the plane, she became keenly aware of how excited and nervous she was. *In 12 hours we'll be in Spain.*

From what sounded like a muffled sound coming from a faraway land, Faith became cognizant that Tina was speaking. "Sorry, what did you say?"

"I asked, 'When will Amanda and Rachael arrive in Hondarribia?'"

"They flew in yesterday. They should be well acclimated to European lifestyle by the time we meet up with them."

"What about the other gals?" Tina asked.

"I think they are coming via Milan."

"Will Amanda and Rachael meet them in Spain before we get there?"

"Are you kidding? You don't think two college kids would want to hang around any of us older gals, do you?"

Tina smiled. "It's going to be great having Amanda with you. I hope to be able to do the same with Lea some day."

"Hey, you two have traveled quite a bit together already. How many times have you been to Italy?"

"Three times, but that's because we have family there."

"Still, you two have such a good relationship. I've always been envious of how much Lea loves you and enjoys being with you."

"Who knows? This trip may be the ticket for you two."

They heard the announcement to board. People with small children rose from their seats. Others gathered their belongings and, either rushed to get in line or meandered to spots to get comfortable and wait for their seat numbers to be called. Tina stood immediately. Faith sat waiting for the line to shorten before rising from her seat.

Before long, Faith and Tina were seated on the plane. With a pillow and blanket in hand, Faith looked around the cabin. She leaned over to Tina and said quietly, "Tina, don't people on international flights look more relaxed than on regular U.S. flights?"

"Maybe, but that's probably because most on this flight are probably going home from a vacation, or like us, going on holiday."

6

HONDARRIBIA

The air was fresh and cool, the sky crystal blue as Faith and Tina's cab drove over the winding mountain road from the airport into Hondarribia. Cliffs abutting beautiful beaches provided a hilly backdrop to the town.

"Isn't this gorgeous?" Tina asked.

"It's got to be one of the most beautiful spots in the world," Faith answered.

When the cab entered an ancient old quarter Faith said, "I feel like we've stepped back in time."

Inside the Hotel Jauregui in Hondarribia they were greeted by a friendly host who apologetically reported their rooms weren't ready.

Still mesmerized by the beauty they had just observed they decided to go explore the small fishing village near the southwestern border of France. Faith asked their host, "Can we leave our bags with you, so we can check out the town?"

"Si senoritas."

As Faith turned to leave, her eyes took in lovely colorful tiles surrounding the front entrance. More pleasing was the view of the sea framed out by the carved, dark wood molding around the open doorway. She smiled viewing small fishing boats bobbing on the crystal blue and turquoise waters.

Lost in thought, she was startled by the sound of a familiar, pleasant voice, "Mom, you made it."

Amanda and Rachael stood in the lobby, comfortable and confident, as if they owned the place. Faith wanted to run to her daughter and hug her tight, but with restraint, she walked slowly to Amanda. But as soon as she reached her daughter all self-control was forgotten, and she hugged Amanda tightly. Rachael and Tina joined them in the warm welcome.

Like a tour guide, Rachael began a summary of the town's wonders on the bay. "We found a wonderful restaurant near the castle of San Telmo. It's like you're in the middle-ages 'a can't-miss' spot."

"Sounds fantastic. I'm starved," Tina said.

"It's almost noon. If we don't eat now, we won't get another chance until late this evening," Amanda said.

As they made their way to the restaurant, Amanda and Rachael took turns revealing highlights of Hondarribia.

"After lunch, it will be too late to see some of the sights, but we could take a stroll along the bay before we go back to the hotel. After our siesta, we can walk to the Castle of San Telmo and, if you're up to it we could also visit the Sanctuary of Nuestra Senora, about three miles from the hotel," Rachael said.

Sitting on the restaurant terrace they viewed immense stone cliffs on the French coastline and ate paella under the spell of friendship and laughter.

After lunch, they went to the bay before returning to their hotel. Tina's pace was so slow that both Amanda and Rachael privately remarked to Faith their concern about Tina's being able to hike the *Camino*.

Faith assured them, "She's just tired from traveling. I'm sure she'll be fine by tomorrow."

After their siesta, rested, they met in the hotel lobby.

"Ready to go?" Amanda asked.

"Ready," Tina and Faith answered enthusiastically.

Rachael, true to her nature, shared historical details as they strolled to the Castle of San Telmo. "The thick, stone walls of the castle formed part of the defensive structure that protected the port of Asturiago."

At the end of the promenade, they stood admiring the castle. "It's spectacular," Faith said.

As they went through the castle's interior, Rachael resumed sharing bits of history. "The castle was built in the 10th century by the King of Navarre in the early days of the Christian re-conquest. It was remodeled in the 16th century by Emperor Charles the Fifth. Noble figures of Europe including Napoleon have stayed in the castle."

Amanda interrupted, "Look at those tapestries and magnificent medieval armor."

"Amazing," Faith responded.

One hour later when they left the castle, Rachael asked. "Is everyone ready to go to the Sanctuary of Nuestra Senora?

To everyone's surprise, Tina said, "We shouldn't wear ourselves out. That would make our trek a six-mile round trip. Let's take a cab."

Faith asked, "Is that okay with you girls?"

Both Amanda and Rachael replied. "That's fine with us."

"By the way, have you two seen the rest of our group?" Faith asked.

"Mom, I'd never met any of them, so we didn't try to connect with them. We figured we'd wait until you got here."

"I'm sure we'll all hook up this evening."

At the Sanctuary, while admiring its rich décor, marvelous plasterwork on its vaults, Rachael reported, "This is one of the most typical Baroque buildings in Cantabria. Since 1605 the Dominican monks have been responsible for its protection. The church was built between 1568 and 1601. In the 17th century, someone tried to steal the statue of Mary. It is said the Blessed Mary made her statue so heavy that it could not be stolen away. The miracle was her way of making it known she would never leave, and would always be there to watch over the town."

By 7:00 p.m. Faith, Tina, Amanda and Rachael had completed their tour of the town and had returned to the hotel. They found the rest of the group lounging in the lobby.

As soon as Jocelyn saw them, she went to Faith and welcomed her to Spain.

"This is Amanda, my daughter, and her friend, Rachael. And this is my friend Tina," Faith said. Jocelyn introduced Honey and Ada. While introductions were made, Faith thought she saw some funny looks pass between them.

"Faith, did you get into town in time to eat?" Jocelyn asked.

"Barely. Eating lunch before siesta is going to be a tough adjustment."

"That's not the hard part. The soonest we can eat dinner is 8:00 p.m. Most places don't serve dinner until 9:00 p.m.," Ada said. "I'm not used to eating so late. Plus, few are early risers in this country. Finding breakfast can be a challenge. Luckily, the hotel had someone bring us rolls and coffee this morning. We'll have to buy breakfast food and snacks at the end of each day, and look for places to eat lunch before siesta time."

Jocelyn piped in, "I bet you'd like to get cleaned up and rest a little before dinner."

Speaking for the group, Faith said, "Yes, and I'm sure the others would as well, but should we talk about tomorrow and where we're going first?"

Jocelyn answered, "We can go over everything at dinner. See you in an hour."

When the others started off to their rooms, Jocelyn asked, "Faith, can we talk?"

"Sure."

Jocelyn looked in Tina's direction, "Alone."

Tina acknowledged the comment, and went to their room.

Faith asked, "Jocelyn, is something wrong?"

"Your friend, Tina is way heavier than I had imagined. She'll never be able to keep up on this trip. Ada and Honey were shocked when they saw her."

"Jocelyn, I told you before we left that we would be going slower, and wouldn't be able to keep up."

In an agitated tone, Jocelyn said, "Yeah, but I had no idea that it was this bad. She'll never be able to do this. We'll never see you. Believe me when I say, I can't spend time worrying about you."

"Calm down, I'm not expecting you to. We'll be fine," Faith said.

Jocelyn gave Faith a look of concern, and then turned away in a huff. "You won't."

When they met for dinner, Faith felt as if Jocelyn avoided her all through the meal. *We haven't walked one step and it looks like there are problems already.*

All of a sudden, Ada blurted out, "Tina, whatever made you think at your weight that you could do this?"

With a soft and serene voice Tina responded, "I'm here on a pilgrimage. I'm not in a race. I am positive that God will give me the strength to do what is needed."

"What's necessary is you should think about going home," Jocelyn said in an antagonistic tone.

Shocked by the reaction of the ladies toward Tina, but not wanting to agitate the situation, Faith said, "I know everyone is concerned about the trip. Tina and I will be fine. We won't be a bother or burden to anyone. Let's eat and get some rest. We'll take it a day at a time."

"Just remember. I've got the directions. Those who don't stick close will be on their own, which is my main concern," Jocelyn said.

"When I asked if I should get maps, you said you'd bring enough for everyone," Faith said.

"I assumed we'd be together. You'll have to get your own."

Faith felt her heartbeat racing. To prevent going ballistic she took a deep breath. After a slow exhale, she asked, "Can we look at your map to see where we are going tomorrow? We'll look for maps tomorrow."

Coolly Jocelyn answered, "I guess." Suddenly her voice rose, "You're ruining my vacation."

Faith shook her head thinking, *I'm sure Jocelyn is concerned for our well being. I just wish she was a little more considerate of Tina's feeling, and wasn't being so controlling.*

Jocelyn shrugged her shoulders. "I just want you to understand, we're not waiting for you."

"No problems," Faith replied.

Tensions lightened through dinner and as they left the restaurant, Faith asked, "Jocelyn, would it be okay to come by your room to jot down directions for tomorrow?"

"Sure."

Jocelyn and Ada dashed in front of Tina and Faith to demonstrate just how good in shape they were. Honey dropped back a slight distance in an attempt to talk and be sociable.

In Jocelyn's room while Faith wrote down directions, conversation remained cordial. Jocelyn relayed helpful tips for finding markers. "Some markers are carved in stone and can be hundreds of years old. Others are newly painted."

Faith forced a smile as she left the room, "Thanks. See you in the morning.'

When Faith returned to her room, she asked Tina, "Are you okay? I'm sorry they behaved so rudely."

"It's okay. You know I'm tough. You can't get a tough girl from New Jersey down. I'm sure after a few days they'll see we are doing fine and things will mellow."

"I hope you're right."

"I can't believe Jocelyn is acting so childish. And I've never seen Ada act like this. I can't believe all this nonsense over maps. I hope we can find a shop where we can purchase maps tomorrow. Asking her each night could be a problem. I better write these instructions down for Amanda. I'm sure the girls will be able to keep up, but just in case they get separated, it would be good for them to have an idea of where they are going."

When Faith finished writing out a second copy of the directions, she climbed into bed. *I sure hope things will be better tomorrow.*

Roman Stone Steps

7

HONDARRIBIA TO SAN SEBASTIAN

Following a second day of sightseeing in Hondarribia, the group met before sunrise. Seven women with weary eyes gathered in the dimly lit lobby. Five were tired from lack of sleep due to the noise of the night's frivolity outside their hotel window. Amanda and Rachael were exhausted from partying with the town most of the night.

Dressed in dry-wick pants and carrying extra tops for layering the group was greeted with a pleasant "*Buenos Dias.*" The young man escorted them to a room set up for breakfast, and directed them to help themselves to the fresh bread and cheese. Then with a charming Spanish accent, asked, "American coffee or cappuccino?" Everyone asked for cappuccinos.

After breakfast, Tina said, "Faith, I'd like to start out before the others. They want to take pictures at the yellow arrow where the *Camino* starts. I don't want to slow them down."

Faith saw a forlorn look on Tina's face. "Is something wrong?"

"I see how everyone looks at me. Like someone as big as me shouldn't be on this pilgrimage."

"Tina, you've already lost weight and are getting stronger every day, just think where you'd be if you weren't on this trip. You may feel people are criticizing of your undertaking, but I believe you are an inspiration. I'm going to find Amanda and tell her that we're heading out."

When Faith rose to leave, she was surprised when a cab driver walked into the breakfast area and Jocelyn greeted him. "Our luggage is at the front desk." Then, she looked at Faith. "Do you gals want to split the carfare with us? We're going to carry only our necessities and send the rest onto San Sebastian."

Caught off guard and skeptical about putting their belongings in a cab Faith, Tina, Amanda and Rachael collectively decided to carry their gear since it was already packed.

After Jocelyn left, Faith looked at the girls and Tina. "Sounds like it could have been a good idea. Wish they had discussed it with us yesterday before we packed up everything. Amanda, can you ask Ada how the cab transfer works, so we can decide if it might work for us tomorrow."

Amanda went to Ada. She returned within minutes and reported, "Ada told me Jocelyn used a cab to carry things on her last two trips and their belongings always arrived safely. Each evening they find a cabdriver nearby and hire him to carry the bags to the next place they're staying. The cab fare averaged $21.00 a day. Ada said if we all share the expense it will be about $3.00 per person. As heavy as these packs are, sending a few items in a cab might be helpful."

Faith nodded, "We'll see how things go today and look into it this evening."

The sun still hadn't peeked over the red-tile roofs tops. Shadows filled the narrow, cobblestone streets as Faith and Tina started out before the others. They walked silently so they wouldn't disturb the sleeping town. While they strolled by quaint and freshly-painted homes and gardens, the rubber tips on their hiking poles tapped rhythmically along the cobblestones.

At the edge of town, when they came to a wooden deck, Faith and Tina saw a Spanish-blue tile with a yellow arrow marking the trail. Within minutes of their discovery, they heard the voices of their group nearby.

From a deck, Faith watched the girls walk out of the fog which lingered in the streets of town. The sight conjured up visions of sorcerers and magic.

Together, the group made their way to a stone bridge. Jocelyn positioned everyone for their photo, making sure the trail's yellow arrow could be seen.

After their photo shoot, for two kilometers, the seven walked together. Then the terrain changed. They started up a steep incline on the way to Santuario de Guadalupe. Jocelyn, Ada, and Honey moved faster.

To keep company with Faith and Tina, Amanda and Rachael maintained a slower pace.

Rachael walked as slowly as she could, and still found herself several feet in front of Tina. She stopped to wait. Faith could she the frustration in Rachael's face and although Amanda was trying hard to hide her feelings, Faith could see that they were going to tire from boredom before the day started.

"Girls, why don't you go ahead? We'll be fine," Faith said.

"You sure you don't mind? We'll wait for you up the road," Amanda said.

"Go on," Faith said.

Over the next two hours, Tina had difficulty catching her breath. The sound of her arduous breathing echoed through the trees.

At one point, Faith and Tina stopped to admire three tall, old, but well-preserved concrete crosses. A directional marker, a clam shell, was carved into the cross closest to the path.

After a short rest, they trekked onward. Another half hour passed ever so slowly before they reached the top of the hill, where a small church stood as a welcoming sight. Even more welcoming was a small café next to the church.

Amanda and Rachael came out of the café, "Mom, Tina, we're all at the café."

"We'll be right there," Faith said. Before joining them, she took a moment to look triumphantly down the path they had just conquered. "Tina, look how steep that hill was. You should be proud. We made it."

Tina nodded, "We did. I need to fill my water pack. It's nearly empty." As she filled it she paused, and said abruptly, "Faith, I wanted to quit."

"I know, but you didn't. Come on, let's get something to eat."

Having already eaten, Jocelyn, Ada, and Honey stood with backpacks on, prepared to leave.

Inside the café, Amanda and Rachael still sat at a table.

Before Honey left the café, she approached Faith's table. "How are you ladies doing? Some hill wasn't it?"

"Sure was," Faith said.

As Jocelyn, Ada, and Honey walked outside, Honey called, "Have a great day."

"Thanks. We will," Tina said.

When Faith and Tina joined Amanda and Rachael, Amanda whispered, "Mom, the owner isn't happy that we're here today. She's not happy having us so-called dirty pilgrims' in her establishment while the townsfolk clientele is dressed for Sunday Mass."

"We won't linger, and you two shouldn't have waited," Faith said.

"Yes, we should have. We didn't want you to miss going into the church and getting our *Camino* Passports stamped. We should all be together, at least, the first time. I want my picture taken getting it signed. Double proof," Amanda answered.

"I hope finding places to get our *Camino* Passports signed along the way will be as easy as today. Without getting it signed each day we won't be able to get our certificate at the end of our pilgrimage," Tina said.

"Tina thanks for doing so much research before the trip. Otherwise, I would not have known to order the *Camino* Passport," Faith said.

"That goes for me too," Amanda said.

"Me too," Rachael chimed in.

"My pleasure," Tina said as she struggled out of her backpack. Rachael placed their orders; they ate, feeling uncomfortable in the shadow of the owner's unhappy glares.

After lunch, they went to the church. With Mass over, a nun with a sweet smile greeted the group at the massive wooden double doors. With compassion, she said to Tina. "This must be very difficult for you." Then, she led them inside the church.

Light streamed through the stained-glass windows and bounced off its gold accents. "It's beautiful," Tina said.

After the tour, the nun invited them into her office. With pride, the four took out their Pilgrim Credentials. The sister signed each Passport, and stamped the *Camino* seal inside, after which they thanked the nun and said their good-byes. Tina turned to the girls, "I guess its back to the road."

When they came to the crossroads Faith and Tina took the winding route which looked as if it would take them more easily over the mountain. Amanda and Rachael chose the path which went straight up a steep slope.

Although the path Tina and Faith selected was more gradual, it rose at an angle that was too narrow and steep for Tina to be confident. Every few steps Tina lost her footing on loose stones. She grabbed tree limbs to keep from falling, while her strained breathing caused Faith to cringe.

With each step, dirt encircled them. The sandy soil no longer held the stones in place. Before long, dust-caked-sweat stuck on their bodies. The weight of the packs grew heavier with each step. Over the next two hours, Tina's breathing became erratic.

"I've got to stop and rest," Tina said.

"I'm thinking we should have checked the cab idea out," Tina said.

"How would we have known we could hire a taxi as a pack mule? I'm sure there will be days where a cab won't be available. But, if the occasion arises tomorrow, we'll do as they did today and lighten our load."

"There's not that much I'd feel safe sending on, maybe toiletries and my extra pair of shoes," Tina said.

"A few less items will give us more room for water and food. We can risk it at a few times and see how it works," Faith said.

Concerned that they were stopping too often and had made such little progress, Faith suggested, "Why don't you take the pack off your back and stretch a little? Maybe if you eat and drink something, it will help."

"I'll never get this pack back on if I take it off."

Faith plopped down to sit, but her own backpack toppled her over into the dirt.

Faith laughed as she regained her balance, "Here, let me help you get that thing off before you fall down, too! Rest. You need to gather your strength."

While Tina rested, Faith took out her rain poncho, spread it on the ground, lay down and, closed her eyes.

Somewhat refreshed, they resumed the climb.

An hour later, about 3:00 p.m., they came to another crossroads, and couldn't find the trail's yellow arrow. Faith looked to the sea, and saw a small fishing village. "Tina, somewhere along the way, we're supposed to take a ferry. Wait here. I'll go down into the village to get directions."

Faith scrambled to the village. It was siesta time. Not a soul was in sight. *What am I to do? Think. You're on the sea. No ferry here. We must need to keep going on the path.*

By the time Faith returned, the redness from over-heating had left Tina's face. "I couldn't find anyone, but there wasn't any sign of a ferry below. We must need to keep on the trail going over the mountain."

Tina protested. "Upward. That can't be right, that direction won't take us to any ferry."

"What do you suggest? I don't think we have any other choice except to keep going."

Reluctantly, Tina agreed.

Over the next half hour, Faith listened to Tina complain about her aching back and sore feet.

They found a spot under a tree and took another break. Faith loosened her shoelaces. She had never felt such foot pain as she did at that moment. The perpetual slipping of feet from walking up and down hills formed blisters on her big toes. When Tina took her shoes off, telltale blood stains on her socks revealed blisters had formed and popped on her feet as well.

As they rested, Faith thought she heard voices. When two hikers appeared on the road, she thought, *It's a miracle.*

In poor Spanish, Faith asked, "Are we on the right path to San Sebastian?"

In English, the hiker replied, "You are still at least four hours from San Sebastian. It's a dangerous path to walk at night."

"But the closest place we can get to is the church," Faith said.

"Yes, the church is much closer. You can get back to the church in less than two hours; long before dark." While listening, Faith calculated. Four hours for them could mean six for them. And if they thought it was two hours back to the church that meant it would take them no less than three.

Faith looked at Tina. *She's exhausted. We're going to have to turn back. She may not even be able to make it back to the church.*

Reluctantly, Faith gave in to what was the only logical choice which was to return to the church. The walk seemed endless. Trudging along, they ran out of food and water.

When they reached the church, the nun was shocked to see them. She took pity and let them come inside. She brought fresh fruit, bread, and water. Then, she called for a cab to take them to the hotel they had booked for that night.

In the cab, Tina said. "Thanks for staying with me, Faith."

"No problem. You'll get stronger each day. Tomorrow will be better."

"I'm not going tomorrow. I'm in too much pain. I need a day to recover. Besides if I take off a day that will give you a chance to be with Amanda."

Faith knew she shouldn't have been surprised. Still, she had mixed feelings. *No matter what, I'm here to support my friend. We will get through this.*

It was 7:30 p.m. when Faith and Tina entered the hotel. Jocelyn and Ada had arrived hours earlier and were sitting in the lobby.

"I see you had to take a cab to find the hotel," Jocelyn said snidely.

Faith pretended not to hear her remark and checked in at the desk.

Jocelyn persisted. "So, what happened to you two?"

"We got a little turned around," Faith said.

"We're all heading out to dinner around 8:00 p.m. Want to join us?" Jocelyn asked.

"We'll get cleaned up and join you." *I'll get Tina settled in our room, then go look for Amanda. I hope Amanda's and Rachael's day was better than ours.*

The room was cramped, held a twin bed, and a pull-out couch. A small window opened to a view of small stoned-walled shops adorned at their entrances by multicolored ceramic pots filled with bright, colorful flowering plants. An ornamental stone fountain flowed in the Town Center Square while lovers snuggled close together on benches.

In their room, Tina took off her backpack, and dropped onto the bed.

Faith examined the room and reported, "We've got a private bath with a tub. I'll shower then fill it with hot water so you can soak."

"I'm not moving for anything. Not to shower, eat, not for any reason."

Faith shook her head in defeat. "I'll be out in a bit."

As soon as Faith closed the door, she sat on a wooden chair in the corner of the closet-sized bathroom. Her head dropped into her hands. She took several deep breaths giving her back time to release the pain before she pulled off her shoes. When the air hit her blisters, the pain magnified. *Never will a shower feel so good.*

When she finished showering and dressed, she filled the tub with warm water and called to Tina, "Tub's ready."

"I'm not getting off this bed," Tina said.

"Where's that strong New Jersey girl?"

"She's hidden under caked sweat and grime, and exhausted," Tina answered.

Faith assisted Tina in removing her shoes. She could see the pain on her face as she loosened her shoelaces.

"Tina, you'll feel better after you soak awhile. I'll bring back something to eat. Just relax."

At the front desk, Faith read Amanda's message. The group was dining at a restaurant only a few blocks away. *I'll get the supplies for tomorrow, join the girls then, bring my dinner and Tina's back to the room.*

Finished with shopping, Faith felt like doing nothing except returning to her room and climbing into bed, but when she saw Amanda's smiling face she was happy she had made the effort to join the group before retreating to her room to dine with Tina.

Amanda and Rachael had saved two seats and were sitting at a large table with the rest of the group.

"How's Tina? Is she okay?" Amanda asked.

"She's fine, just exhausted."

Honey laughed softly. "I hope you're not thinking that the rest of us are full of energy. I've never been so tired. I'm rooming with Ada down the hall from you. If you need anything just come and knock on the door."

"I think we'll be fine, but thanks for the offer," Faith said.

Tina had showered and was resting comfortably when Faith returned with dinner. "Dinner is served."

Tina got out bed and sat in a chair. "Smells wonderful."

No sooner had they finished eating than Tina was back in bed. Within minutes she was under the covers sound asleep.

Faith looked in her bag and realized she was out of blister pads. She walked down to Amanda's room and knocked on the door. Rachael answered. "Amanda's in the bathroom. She'll be out soon. How's Tina?"

"She's sleeping soundly. She has some awful blisters on her feet and so do I."

"We bought some wonderful blister protectors. Jocelyn and the others purchased something called, Compead. It's like a Band-aid with a pain reliever that doesn't rub off. We bought enough for you and Tina, just in case."

"Great. How did your day go?"

"It was sort of strange. When we'd catch up to the others, they'd speed up. We like to stop to check things out. Eventually, they were too far ahead for us to walk with, but we didn't have any difficulties finding our way," Rachael answered.

"Did you get into town early enough to visit the Buen Pastor Cathedral?" Faith asked.

"It was late, but we took a quick look. I found a brochure that said it was built in 1877 from sandstone from Monte Igueldo quarries, designed by the architect Manuel de Echave, and the glass stained windows were made by Juan Bautista Lazaro."

With a touch of frivolity in the tone of her voice, Faith said, "Rachael, I hope you're writing this stuff down or saving all these brochures you're picking up. By the end of this trip you'll have a hard time keeping all these churches and cathedrals straight in your mind, much less remember them."

Amanda popped out of the bathroom. "Mom, do you think Tina will be able to walk tomorrow?"

"I hope so. She's in rough shape, but she's no quitter, and this pilgrimage means so much to her. She gave me my marching instructions before we left for Spain. No matter what, I am not to let her quit. I made her that promise. She yells a lot, but it's just an Italian thing."

"We'll check in before we leave in the morning. We've bought bottled water, juice and fruit for you. We also bought blister pads."

"Rachael already gave me the pads. Thanks for everything else, too."

Faith hugged the girls. "Tina will be relieved. Her feet are bloody awful. See you in the morning."

"Mom, I know you feel confident that Tina will walk tomorrow, but what if she can't," Amanda asked.

With a soft look of concern on her face, Faith answered, "She could go in the cab with the luggage to the next hotel, but I'm sure she'll be fine by morning."

Camino Marker

8

SAN SEBASTIAN TO ZARAUTZ

In that moment before the sun rose and night turned into day, Faith rolled over on the sofa bed. The mattress was so soft she had to grab the corner to prevent a fall. Coming into consciousness, Faith heard Tina fumbling through her suitcase. *Tina's awake. I wonder what she's going to do.*

"Tina, what time is it?"

"It's only 6:00 a.m."

"Do my eyes deceive me? You're up already? Did you fall out of bed?"

"Sort of, I'm not feeling too bad. I'm going with you today. I figure if I get tired I can catch a cab."

"We might not come to a town where you can catch a cab. Are you willing to risk it?"

"I am. After all, today the load will be lighter with us sending part of our things ahead in the cab. Honey said that the distance is shorter today. I figure we probably walked as far as they did, since we backtracked so much."

Relieved at Tina's decision, Faith dressed and went to breakfast.

After breakfast, the entire group brought their bags to the roadside to be sent by cab to their next destination. With 15 years of experience supervising staff at a large New York law firm, Ada took command, and gave the cab driver directions on where to deliver their bags in Zarautz.

As soon as the bags were in the cab, all seven went to find the *Camino* markers at the start of the day's trail. Ada and Jocelyn led the group. Honey joined Rachael and Tina. Faith and Amanda walked behind them.

For half an hour, they strolled past beautiful, older homes and buildings. "Mom, aren't the flower gardens and flowers in window boxes pretty?" Amanda asked.

"Beautiful. I love how the flowers stand out against the white buildings. I'm going to miss, San Sebastian," Faith said.

At the outskirts of town, the sidewalk took them to a pathway that traveled along side a massive rock formation. Jocelyn was the first to round the corner, and spot the stone *Camino* marker pointing toward the stone stairway. Jocelyn moved quickly to lead the way. Ada followed close behind.

Jocelyn called out, "Honey, better get a move on."

Honey looked at Tina and Rachael, smiled, and shrugged her shoulders. "Can't keep the queen waiting. I'll see you gals later, hopefully for lunch." Honey moved quickly to catch Jocelyn and Ada, and thought, *I should walk with Amanda and Rachael, that way I'd get to know them better.* She took a deep breath. *Coming up with a plan is not going to be as easy as I thought.*

At the top of the ridge, Jocelyn stopped, leaned over the edge, and yelled. "Tina, better start saying your 'Hail Mary's.' Those steps are hell."

When Faith and Tina turned a corner they saw what Jocelyn meant. In front of them were an endless number of steps going straight up the side of the mountain. No end to these steps could be seen.

Tears formed in Tina's eyes, as she whimpered, "Faith I can't do this. It's too steep for me. The steps are uneven heights and there are no handrails."

"You can do it. Don't look up. Put one foot in front of the other, and don't think about the next step. Just take it one step at a time."

The Roman stone stairway took them up through thick brush, and under grapevines as large as oak trees. Wiping sweat from their brows, breathing hard, and stepping gingerly along the *Camino* path they pushed upward. Twice they passed medieval ruins lost in time amongst vineyards.

As they walked the path over the mountain range, strolling under the branches of the vines, hundreds of bunches of lush grapes dangled above their heads.

When they came upon a worker in the vineyard, they asked to buy a bunch of grapes. The caretaker smiled, pulled two large red bunches of grapes off a vine and gave each of them a bunch. Faith tried to give him some money. He shook his head. *"Bon Camino."*

At a wide shelf of rock, Faith and Tina rested and took time to enjoy the sweet, fresh grapes. They looked over the mountain range they had traveled. The town they'd left that morning embraced the sea and looked like a pinprick nestled amid a patchwork of patterns and colors of vineyards and farms below. Exhausted from the climb, the beauty that lay before them gave them the energy needed to continue.

From that point, the road continued uphill, but leveled slightly helping to ease the pull of gravity on their backpacks.

Out of vineyards, the path transitioned into open fields and farms. They were surprised when they came to a barbed-wire fence in the middle of a field. There wasn't a gate anywhere to be seen. The fence was too low and tight to allow them to scoot under it or in between the wire, and too high to climb over.

Tina and Faith stood looking at a stepstool by the fence.

"Guess this stool is for us pilgrims," Tina said, as she pointed to the yellow arrow painted on a tree on the other side of the fence.

After taking off her backpack and tossing it over the fence, Tina using the stepstool for balance sat on the wider than normal fence post. She then swung her legs around to the other side, and waited for Faith to maneuver the stepstool through the wire and position it so she could balance and get to the ground. After Tina had made it over the fence, Faith went over, and then, put the stepstool back in its original place.

As they continued their trek, they happily found the next few fences intersecting the trail, all had gates.

At the edge of a meadow they came to a roadside stand. The handwritten sign stapled to a wooden board offered pilgrims to take water from a fountain. They filled their water containers.

"Look, there's a place to sign our names and stamp our *Camino* passports," Tina said.

They stamped their *Camino* passports, and after a short break, resumed their journey. Eventually, the incline leveled out, but uneven surfaces forced their ankles to twist, and their feet burned whenever rocks poked into the soles of their shoes.

Tina lowered her head. "I'm so tired."

Faith pointed to a sign. "We're close to the city of Orio. We're nearing today's halfway mark. That means lunch."

At a charming open-air restaurant, they sat outside away from other patrons. They ordered Cokes and the day's special. Kicking off their shoes, Faith felt all was well until Tina announced, "I'm taking a cab from here to Zarautz."

"But we've already made it this far. You can make it," Faith said.

"Nope. If I go any farther, I won't be able to walk tomorrow. My feet are already swollen. I'm never going to be able to get my shoes on again."

Frustrated, Faith said, "I'll go with you, and then backtrack from the hotel. That way I'll meet up with the group, and spend some time with Amanda."

When Faith got into the cab, she wanted to scream. She wished Tina would stick it out. She felt sure she could do it.

At the hotel, Faith asked the desk clerk, "I'd like to walk the *Camino* backwards. Where does it come into town?

The clerk was surprised at her question. "You want to walk it backwards?"

"Yes," Faith answered. "My friends are on the path and I'd like to go meet them."

The clerk gave her directions, and as Faith followed the path back to join her daughter, she realized that traveling the route in reverse was making it impossible to see the directional arrows.

The path leveled off and wove through a wide grassy meadow. A welcome breeze cooled her hot face, and she could smell the salt-ocean air. Her shoulders relaxed. *I'm alone. How wonderfully peaceful this is.*

Faith recalled a day when Amanda asked Eagle Claw, her Cherokee elder friend, "Does God speak to you when you're meditating?"

With a wisp of a smile, he answered, "I'm not sure whether it's God I hear, or, if in the stillness and quiet, I hear my own thoughts. What I do know is unless you sit in silence, you will never hear God or know your-self."

Thinking about Eagle Claw's statement, she wondered, when was the last time she was alone? When was the last time she had heard her own thoughts? She concluded, it had been too long.

Now, enjoying the moment, and keenly aware of the sound of the breeze brushing against her skin, she took a deep breath to enjoy the sweet scent of wild flowers. She was on a pilgrimage. It was her time to be with God in all His glory.

Off in the distance, she heard the sound of familiar voices. *Guess it is back to reality.*

As expected, Jocelyn and Ada were the first to crest the hill. Bowled over by her sudden appearance, Jocelyn asked. "Faith, how did you get ahead of us?"

In a flustered tone, Ada said. "Jocelyn, she can explain later. We need to tell her about Amanda."

Alarmed Faith asked, "What happened to Amanda? Is she okay?

"She's okay, but she had us worried for awhile. Right after lunch, her throat closed, her face swelled and blew up like a balloon, and she couldn't breathe. Fortunately, she had Benedryl with her which Rachael pulled out of her backpack and gave to her. Without that medicine, I'm not sure we could have gotten help in time. We weren't near a pharmacy, and I'm sure we couldn't have found a doctor," Ada said.

"Where is she now?" Faith asked.

"She's not far behind. Rachael is with her, and Honey stayed back as a precaution," Ada said.

"Thanks," Faith said, and set out at a quickened pace along the path to find Amanda.

Honey trekked alongside Amanda. "I gather you've had a reaction to shellfish in the past."

"Yep, in fact, when I was only seven years old, I nearly died. We didn't live close to a hospital, but Mom got me to a doctor in time."

While listening, Honey devised a plan. If Amanda ate shrimp unknowingly and didn't have her allergy medication with her, she'd be a goner. "I bet your father must have been real upset, too," Honey said.

"He was out of town."

"He must be worried about you and Faith now, trekking off to Spain."

Honey watched Amanda's facial features become drawn. The tone of her voice softened. "He died a couple of years ago."

"So sorry," Honey said.

Honey looked down the path and was stunned to see Faith walking toward them.

As soon as Faith was within ear range of the other girls, she said, "Before you ask, I went with Tina to the hotel and decided to walk back to meet you girls."

Faith turned to Amanda. "I hear I missed some excitement. Jocelyn and Ada gave me their report, but I'd like to hear it from you."

"I ordered what I thought was vegetable soup. It turned out to have a small amount of shrimp in it for flavoring, and you know how allergic I am to shrimp. But I'm fine now. The swelling went down pretty quickly after I took the Benadryl you packed for me. Good thing you thought about that."

"You've got to be careful about what you eat."

"I will. How's the path look into town?" Amanda asked.

"It's not too bad, except the stairwell into town is a bit of a challenge."

Rachael laughed, "Does that surprise anyone?"

"Not me," Honey said.

Amanda's smiled, "Me neither."

Honey purposely walked with Faith, leaving some separation between them and Rachael and Amanda.

"Honey, thanks for staying with the girls."

"My pleasure. They're good kids."

"Is there anything I should know about Amanda's incident?" Faith asked.

"Not really. Amanda knew what to do, but Rachael seemed shaken by the event."

"How are you enjoying the trip so far?" Faith asked.

"I have to admit it's much tougher than I expected. But from experience, I know the pain should lessen as our bodies get used to it."

"I hope you're right. My big toes are killing me."

Honey thought, *Good*, behind her friendly smile.

Finally reaching the top of the ridge, the four gathered before their descent into town. The wind rippled the grass on the rolling hills, and the vastness of the ocean below dwarfed the appearance of the city below.

"How far is the hotel from here?" Rachael asked.

"It's probably only a mile once we're off the path. We got lucky today. The hotel is adorable although it's more like a bed and breakfast. The beds look comfy, and the owner said she's going to fix us dinner tonight and breakfast in the morning."

"And how about Tina? How's she doing? Really doing?" Honey asked.

"Honestly, I feel that once she finishes a full day's trek, she'll have the confidence to take on a full day."

Amanda put her hand on her mother's shoulder. "Mom, maybe tomorrow will be the day."

Pretending to be concerned, Honey asked, "And Faith, how are you doing?"

Faith had not had an opportunity to talk freely about her concerns. She wanted to blurt out that if she didn't feel responsible for Amanda, Rachael and Tina, she would be heading home. But she thought better of sharing her concerns. Honey was Jocelyn's friend, and she didn't want anything she said to be repeated or misinterpreted.

Faith smiled and answered, "I'm fine."

At the end of the path, they came to a crudely-paved road that spiraled down into town. Amanda pointed to the coastline along the beach. "Mom, aren't those mansions magnificent?"

"There are some gorgeous homes in this town. Wait until you see the place where we will be staying," Faith said. "It's beautiful."

Rachael looked at the sea, and with joy in her voice, said, "Wow. Look those guys are surfing. The Jersey Shore never looked this good."

Faith laughed, "This town is known for its famous cooking schools. It must be all that good food that makes those boys look so healthy."

"That's silly, but I wouldn't mind checking out one of those schools. Do you think we'll have time to visit a cooking school? Plus, I'd also like to see the church, Santa Maria la Real? It's supposed to be a great example of a Romanesque structure," Rachael said.

"I don't see why not," Faith said.

In town, the streets were lined with Basque-style buildings, taller than others they had encountered in the more remote areas.

Faith pointed down the street to a quaint, beautifully landscaped, two-story building. That's home for tonight. Amanda and Rachael ran to the front door and stopped at opposite sides of the door, bowed like bellmen greeting guests. Amanda invitingly said, "Welcome to our humble abode."

Inside, the owner smiled, and guided them to their rooms. "Your friends have already arrived."

After the room arrangements were set, the innkeeper asked, "Is there anything I can get you?"

Honey, speaking for the group, answered, "Nothing just now, thanks." In her room she found Ada comfortable in a chair reading a book.

Ada looked up. "Finally made it in? How's Amanda?"

"She's good."

"Dinner is in the dining room at eight. I'm looking forward to a real home-cooked Spanish meal," Ada said.

"Me, too."

Later that evening when the group met for dinner, they found the table was set with fine china and fresh flowers. Wonderful aromas of fresh bread, salad topped with anchovies, baked chicken and boiled potatoes made Honey's mouth water.

When everyone was seated, the innkeeper's wife brought carafes of white and red wine to the table. "Please, eat and enjoy."

Dinner conversation remained pleasant throughout the main meal, but when the flan dessert arrived. "Tina, are you walking tomorrow or taking another vacation day?" Jocelyn asked.

Tina calmly answered, "I'm feeling good. And, the answer to your question is. Yes. I'm going to give it a try. "

"You mean, try, like today. Take a cab?" Jocelyn said indignantly.

Before Tina had a chance to answer, Rachael interrupted. "Aren't we scheduled for a day off soon?"

"Two days, then we'll get a day off," Faith answered.

Tensions relaxed and conversation turned to the pleasantries of the day.

Coastal View

9

ZARAUTZ TO GERNIKA

The days from Zarautz to Markina-Xemein were fatiguing for the entire group. Yet, after facing challenges from feet blistering to extreme climbs, Tina managed to walk every step from Zarautz to Deba, and from Deba to Markina-Xemein. Faith couldn't have been more pleased with her progress. Additionally, Faith's hopes were encouraged when at the end of the day, in spite of her and Tina's usual late arrival; the group would celebrate heartily Tina's success.

Now, getting ready to leave Markina-Xemein for Gernika, following a night of song and dance, Faith wished she had called it a night sooner. She looked out the window of their room and noticed that even the cats were still comfortably sleeping on tin roofs. A rooster crowed, and a dog raised his head slowly as if to complain, then, lowered it as if to say, it wasn't worth the effort.

The entire group started off together. The sun shown brightly while they stepped gingerly over centuries old, Roman curved stones tightly packed with a cement mixture of broken tiles and sand. The stones were designed to allow the runoff off water, but now they were worn so slick pilgrims had to watch their step as they walked the 'Roman way.' Before long Faith and Tina, traveling at a slower pace, once again were separated from the rest of the group.

Tina fearful of slipping kept her hiking pole moving securely in front of her with each step she took.

"The Romans created roads like these all over the western world to move armies and trade goods. I can't believe how often we run into them in these remote areas," Faith said.

"Yeah, I'm not sure whether I like the paved roads or dirt better. As long as it's not raining, they both seem okay, and when it's raining we either sink into mud or slip over rock. Doesn't seem to make a lot of difference," Tina said.

The mountain path took an 18% grade upward, and Tina's breathing became erratic, "I can't breath. I'm going back."

Faith anxious that Tina's heart might give out suggested they stop and rest. "It won't be long before the path levels and we start back down the mountain. I'll go ahead and look for the next yellow arrow. Rest. I'll be back in a few."

When Faith returned she reported, "We're almost at the peak. Take it slow and easy. We'll be there before you know it."

Tina's breathing returned to normal. Faith breathed a sigh of relief.

When they reached the top of the mountain, Faith suggested they rest again before going on. She pulled a small bag that held a blue poncho out of her backpack and tossed it down on the ground under the shade of a tree. It opened up into a big circle.

Tina opened her poncho and laid it out on the ground. "These ponchos are huge. If it rains they will cover our whole body without even having to take the backpack off. So far, the rains have come at night. We've faced wet ground and slippery stones, but haven't had to walk in the rain."

Faith and Tina took off their hiking vests, and folded them to use as pillows. Comfortable on their backs with their heads propped on their fabricated pillows, they looked up through the tree branches. The cool breeze stirred the leaves.

"How beautiful, the sun's rays look like diamonds twinkling on the leaves," Faith said.

While taking deliberate slow breaths, Faith closed her eyes. *I'll rest my eyes for a minute or two.* She counted backwards repeatedly from 8 to 1 in attempts to keep negative thoughts from creeping into her consciousness. *8, 7, 6, 5, 4, 3, 2, 1. . . It's a beautiful day. 8, 7, 6, 5. . . .*

Sometime later, Faith was startled awake.

"Hey, better get up if you want to get to Gernika before dark," Tina said.

"How long have I been asleep?"

"I have no idea. I dozed off, too."

Sitting with their backs to the tree, they viewed the expanse in front of them. In the valley below, they could see a cluster of homes with red-brick roofs.

"Faith, do you think that's where we will be staying?"

Faith suspected the city would be located on the coast, near the water, but unsure, she answered, "It could be. Guess we better get moving."

A short distance down the road, the path leveled and started on a gradual decline. The wall of rock alongside the road was covered with blue and purple hydrangeas.

"Have you ever seen hydrangeas this big? Each flower is almost as big as a soccer ball. I've never seen them so colorful and growing wild. It looks as if they are traveling to the clouds," said Tina.

"In case you hadn't noticed we are in the clouds."

"Faith, Honey asked me about Carl. It took me by surprise. Honey said Amanda had brought him up in conversation."

"What did you tell her?"

"Not much. I told her he died a couple of years ago and Amanda took it hard."

Faith took a deep soulful breath. "Tina, I'm sure the others have shared all the gory details with her by now. And who knows how they told the story. You know, I still feel Amanda blames me. She's acting better, but she'll never understand what really happened. And in some ways, I feel its better, she doesn't."

"Honey was probably just curious. I'm sorry I mentioned it."

"I'm glad you did," Faith said, then raised her head and looked off into the distance. "Listen. Do you hear that?"

"Sounds like a cow's bell. There's more than one cow out there with a bell. We must be getting close to a town," Tina said.

"Maybe we'll find a place to get something to eat."

After walking a short distance, they came to a small village, only to discover shops and restaurants were closed.

"When we walk through these towns and the people are taking their siestas, it feels like we are passing through ghost towns," Tina said.

"It is strange, but the smell of flowers gives you a hint, that people live here."

"It's not the aroma of flowers that intrigues me right now. It's the scent of the veggies in the gardens. I'm starved," Tina said.

"Have you noticed how different the landscape is today from yesterday?" Faith asked.

"Yep. We haven't seen anything like that continuous rock strata we hiked along side of yesterday. It was called 'flysch', wasn't it?" Tina asked.

"That's what I read," Faith answered. "The church of San Pedro in Zumania was interesting too. We were lucky to reach the city during the hours the church was open. Cooling down inside was great. I enjoyed reading about its Gothic design, and seeing Juan de Antxieta's sculpture. The brochure said his sculpture is the only work by a Basque sculptor in the province of Guipuzcoa." She sighed. "But, it looks as if we aren't going to find a place here to rest or to get a bit to eat. Maybe, in the next town we'll find someplace open?" Faith pointed to a stone-wall. "We can sit over there for a few minutes before heading out. I have some crackers and a couple of apples."

After a short break, the path took them out of the village and wandered along small country one-lane roads through farmlands and another sleeping hamlet.

Five hours later, they crested a hill. Below they could see Gernika.

With agony written all over her face, Tina pulled out the hotel's address from her pack, "I hope the hotel is close. We need to be sure where we are going. I don't want to add an extra block."

After making only one wrong turn, an hour later, they arrived at the hotel. Amanda was sitting on a bench in front of the hotel waiting. When she saw them, she stood and greeted them. "We were worried. We ran out of food and water. We didn't find anyplace to get anything, and figured you didn't either. We were about to go back and bring you supplies."

"We had enough supplies with us to get us through most of the day, but I sure am thirsty," Tina reported.

Near the hotel's entrance, the rest of the group sat at tables in the square. Amanda directed Faith and Tina to the square. After they joined the others and were seated they enjoyed sandwiches while hydrating happily with cool water followed by glasses of wine.

"Mom, we've already brought your bags to your room. Let us take your packs. Sit and rest."

Smiles replaced lines of fatigue on Tina's and Faith's faces.

Jocelyn joined them at their table and asked, "So Tina, which part did you skip today?"

Faith started to rise from her seat. A look from Tina stopped her.

Tina smiled at Jocelyn. "I made it the whole way." She paused, "Again."

In a high-pitched tone, Faith asked, "Jocelyn, what's with the attitude?"

"No attitude." Jocelyn looked at Tina. "Good job. By the way, we're meeting in the lobby at 8:00 p.m. this evening to go to a restaurant recommended by the hotel's proprietor. If you've recovered by then, we'll see you."

"We don't need to meet up with them. A later supper would be okay for us," Amanda said.

"I'm feeling pretty good now," Tina said. "I'm not going to let them stop me from going to a well-recommended restaurant. We'll meet them at 8:00."

Later, they strolled along narrow, cobblestone streets lined with old stone buildings to get to the restaurant. On the way, Rachael read from her tour book. "We are in the Viscaya Region noted for its spectacular ocean views. I bet few have seen views such as we have seen while walking these mountain paths. My guidebook states the town center was founded in 1355 by Don Tello. He was the illegitimate brother of Pedro 'The Cruel.' They don't say much about Pedro, or why he was called 'The Cruel.'"

Inside the restaurant, Faith found the setting totally agreeable. It was quaint, and the arrangement was two tables, for two groups.

At Faith's table, the young waiter greeted them with a warm smile, "*Buenos noches, senoritas. Vino?*"

In Spanish, Tina requested, "*Vino rozo, per favor.*"

In minutes, bread, wine and water were brought to the table, and dinners were ordered. While Amanda poured everyone a glass of wine, she said, "I can't wait until tomorrow." Her voice rose, "We get a day off. This getting to bed so early to walk early the next day is getting old. I want to stay out some evenings and mingle."

Tina rolled her eyes, "Amanda, we haven't been walking even a week. And we haven't called it a night before 11:00 p.m. since we started. And you girls have stayed out later most evenings. I can't imagine you two are missing much."

"But it's so tiring," Amanda whimpered.

When they finished their dinners, they thanked their waiter. With satisfied pride, he brought the bill. As usual, it was close to 11:00 p.m.

After Tina turned in, Faith found she was too churned up inside to end the day. *I think I'll get a nightcap in the square before turning in.*

Honey heard Faith's door open and close. *I wonder who's stepping out this late.* When she opened her door, she saw Faith heading toward the lobby. She dressed and stepped outside. Faith sat at a table in front of the hotel overlooking the square. *This is my chance to try to get closer.* Honey boldly went to Faith's table. "Trouble sleeping?"

"Yeah. I guess I ate too much."

"I ordered a glass of wine. Want to join me?" Faith asked.

"Love to."

"Are you worried about Tina?" Honey asked.

"Not so much anymore. I'm getting used to things being up in the air everyday. I'm looking at these unexpected changes as mechanisms for adventure. I'm learning not to worry about what others think. Tina and I have been friends for a long time. She's going through a lot right now. Besides, we manage to get in quite a few laughs throughout a day and the landscape is so beautiful, it offsets most difficulties."

"I've noticed Amanda and Rachael seem to be having fun." At the very moment Honey finished her comment, they saw Amanda and Rachael flirting with two boys by the statue on the square.

"Yep, it looks like they're having fun," Honey giggled, "Sorry, I couldn't help it."

Faith smiled, "No problem. They're young, and I'm glad to see they are enjoying themselves."

"Want to surprise them?" Honey asked.

"Why not?"

Handsome young men played their guitars at the center of the square. One sat on the steps, another stood leaning against the base of a statue. Amanda and Rachael sat at a table directly in front of the entertainers, drinking wine and smiling. They didn't even notice when Faith and Honey came up to their table.

"Enjoying the music?" Faith asked.

Rachael flinched, surprised to hear English being spoken nearby. After the voice registered in her mind, she smiled, "We sure are. It's about time you got out. Pull up a couple of chairs. There is a waitress circulating taking orders. I'll find her and get a couple of glasses. We're drinking red wine. Is that okay? Or would you like something else?"

Faith looked at Honey, "Is red okay with you?"

"Red's fine. Looks like you're enjoying the music and the view as well."

With a tilt of her head and a wisp of a smile, Amanda said, "They are cute, but can you believe all that is going on in this square? Look over there. Kids are tossing balls; others are pushing dolls in baby carriages while their parents dance to the music. And, what's more amazing is that the older people are in the square too, playing cards, talking and enjoying the music. Every night in every town, the village folk are out enjoying each others company. It seems every age group in the U.S. has its own hanging-out places. And, most elderly don't frequent the same places the younger groups do."

The young guitar player stood, and was joined by his friend. They strolled through the square as they sang their way to Amanda's table. When they finished their song, one spoke briefly to Rachael in Spanish. Rachael interpreted. "Some of their friends are sitting at a table over there." She pointed, and then, looked at Faith, "Would it be a problem if we leave you two to join them?"

"Go have fun," Faith said.

Amanda started to walk away then returned to the table. "Mom, it's good to see you out. And that goes for you too, Honey. Have fun and watch out for those guys sitting two tables away. They have their eyes on you."

After the girls left, Honey said, "They really are good kids. Amanda is a doll. It must be a joy to have a daughter that you are so close to."

"Our relationship has been a little strained over the last few years, but things are getting better. How about you? Married? Kids?"

"I was married but it didn't work out. No kids came out of it. Thank goodness."

"Anyone special now?" Faith asked.

Honey felt heat rise to her face. She felt it would be best the less Faith knew of her personal life and answered, "Not right now." Honey paused a moment before continuing, "Amanda told me her father died a couple of years ago. Were you and your husband close? If I'm talking out of turn, just tell me to shut up."

Faith suspected that Jocelyn and Ada had been gossiping about Carl's murder, and she really didn't feel like explaining anything at the moment. Yet, she liked Honey. So instead of brushing her off, she answered, "It's a long story, and I'd rather not delve into it too deeply right now. The short version is, Amanda was kidnapped. I was instructed to come to her alone. However, I told my ex-husband, and he came to our rescue. He died saving our lives."

Honey's curiosity increased. She wanted to ask questions about the kidnapping. She desperately wanted to catch Faith in a lie regarding Ivan, but she knew this was not the appropriate time. With restraint, she replied, "It's getting late, even for some Spaniards. I can't believe it, but it's already 2:00 a.m. in the morning. Good thing we can sleep-in tomorrow. Ready to head back?"

Faith sighed, "Sure."

While heading to their rooms, Amanda and Rachael came up behind them, and Amanda asked, "Did you enjoy your night out?"

Faith and Honey answered, "Sure did."

Amanda spoke in a low tone, and with great enthusiasm injected, "And we have a day off. Yeah!"

Faith shook her head, "Good night, you two."

To prevent waking Ada, Honey gently closed the door to their room, *This is hell, not being able to call Ivan.* She wished she could call him to let him know of her progress. Getting close to Faith and Amanda without creating friction with Jocelyn was a problem that she hadn't counted on. She thought on a trip like this everyone would be getting along. At least this evening, inroads had been made between her and Faith. Still she was finding it more and more difficult to be pleasant to Faith.

Shrine of Miguel

10

GERNIKA TO LEZAMA

In the morning, before deciding to get out of bed Honey waited until she heard Ada leave their hotel room to join Jocelyn. She reviewed topographical maps of the land they would travel and possible towns for stopovers the next few days. She decided Sunday would be the best day to poison Amanda. Stores and restaurants would be closed. It would be a long day and they would travel through few towns.

Feeling comfortable with her plan, Honey rolled over and went back to sleep.

An hour later, people talking and the aroma of fresh- brewed coffee lured Honey to her feet. After she dressed and left the room her first stop was to order a breakfast of cheese, bread and Café con Leche. While sitting in a courtyard square her food was served by a young man, *I'm going to miss this wonderful coffee. I'm going to have to get me a cappuccino maker.* She smiled, *But where am I going to get these cute young men to make it and bring it to me.* Next, she visited a local grocery store suggested by the hotel manager. To Honey's pleasure, the two main ingredients she needed to complete her plan were available, peanut butter and orange marmalade. The other necessary ingredient, shrimp, would always be readily available along the way.

Faith, Tina, Amanda and Rachael had also slept in late. Upon waking, each performed her usual routine of washing clothes so they could dry before repacking, then, met in the lobby.

"Is everyone ready to go for a walk? The Church of Santa Maria is about a half an hour from here. I'm sure we'll find a restaurant along the way," Faith said.

"Are you trying to be funny? What other choice do we have but to go for a walk," Tina said.

On their way out of the hotel, they saw Honey returning. "Honey, we're heading for breakfast and to see the Church of Santa Maria. Want to join us?" Faith asked.

"Sure. I've already eaten, but I could stand another cup of coffee. Just let me drop this stuff in my room. Have you been to the farmer's market yet?"

"Not yet. We planned to stop on our way back," Faith said.

"I'll be right back."

After breakfast, Rachael took her usual role of docent at the church. "The church of Santa Maria is an excellent example of neoclassic design combining both Greek and Egyptian elements."

Amanda walked down the center aisle. Midway to the altar she stopped to gaze upon its beauty. "Well, whoever carved those walls and statues and adorned them with gold had a lot of talent."

"And patience," Tina added.

The five sat in the front row of the church, silently admiring the workmanship on the altar. Without anyone stating it was time to continue, they stood up in unison. They strolled along the inside perimeter of the church, stopping at each small alcove created to honor a Saint or the Blessed Virgin. For the next hour, the only words spoken among them were in awe to praise the amazing artistic details in the paintings, statues, and architecture.

After being in the dim light for so long when they stepped outside the church the sun temporarily blinded them. "Mom, would you like me and Rachael to get your supplies so you can rest before lunch?"

"That would be wonderful," Faith answered.

"What about you, Honey? Do you need anything or are you ready to head back?" Faith asked.

"I'd like to go to the market with the girls, if they don't mind the company."

"That's fine with us," Amanda said.

"Tina, can you make your way back on your own? I'd like to visit the Rock Church. There shouldn't be too many visitors there at this hour. I've been missing my meditation time and thought this would be a good time and place," Faith said.

"No problem. I'll catch up with you later at the hotel."

When Faith entered the Rock Church she was astonished by the center placement of the rocks and the Shrine of San Miguel de Arretxinaga. She sat on a bench and stared in wonder. She had read that the large rocks were more than 40-million-years old, but it was how they had been linked together to form a chapel that was so amazing. *The shrine looks surreal. It looks as if San Miguel is actually standing there praying.*

Faith closed her eyes, took deep rhythmic breaths, and began counting backwards from 8 to 1. Before long, she was lost in a profound, uninterrupted silence, and found magnificent peace. An hour later when she opened her eyes, she thanked God and quietly recited the prayer of St. Francis.

> Lord, make me an instrument of your peace.
>
> Where there is hatred, let me sow love;
>
> where there is injury, pardon;
>
> where there is doubt, faith;
>
> where there is despair, hope;
>
> where there is darkness, light;

and where there is sadness, joy.

O Divine Master, grant that I may not so much seek

to be consoled as to console;

to be understood as to understand;

to be loved as to love.

For it is in the giving that we receive;

It is in the pardoning that we are pardoned;

and it is in dying, that we are born to eternal life.

Amen

Well, God, I asked to go on a pilgrimage and here I am. If this trip doesn't strengthen my spiritual understanding, nothing will. Every step, every challenge has brought me joy in a surprising way and closer to finding my center, and You. Whatever is Your will for me on this journey; thanks for keeping us safe.

Basilica of Begona, Bilboa

11

LEZAMA TO BILBAO

The hike to the outskirts of Bilbao had taken ten hours. Blisters on Faith's and Tina's feet were screaming. Now, they stood at the edge of the city staring down a mile of medieval steps that would take them to what they hoped would be a modern, contemporary hotel.

"I hope our hotel is close. It could still be miles to our hotel looking at the size of this city. I'm not sure how much farther I can go," Tina said.

"Just focus on two days of relaxing," Faith said.

After they navigated the steps into Bilbao they passed through narrow streets and old-world buildings in the older section. When they entered the modern section of the city they found the setting very similar to what you would find in New York City. People were dressed in up-to-date clothing and stared at them covered in dirt, carrying backpacks, tapping hiking poles as if they were strange aliens from another planet. Cars honked and buses roared. Having left the quiet and peace of the *Camino* trail, Faith found the noise of the city upsetting. All that changed as soon as they entered the Sheraton Hotel and found refuge inside.

It had taken them an additional two hours to reach the hotel. At 9:00 p.m. the sun was now just setting.

The desk clerk greeted them warmly, "Your luggage is in your room. We hope you enjoy your stay."

For the first time in days, Faith found Tina's smile genuine as she thanked the young man behind the desk and asked, "Could you schedule a massage for me and my friend tomorrow?"

"With pleasure. I'll call your room as soon as I have available times. She will come to your room."

"How late is your restaurant open?" Faith asked.

"We serve dinner until 1:00 a.m."

"Great. Do you have laundry service?" Faith asked.

"We do. And it is very reasonable."

"Thanks. Can you ring my daughter's room, Amanda Straton? I'd like to let her know we've arrived."

He rang Amanda's room and handed Faith the phone.

Faith smiled when she heard her daughter's contented voice, "Mom, this place is heavenly. We've sent our clothes out to be cleaned. And, guess what I found? Maps!"

Faith laughed, "That's great. Have you eaten?"

"Yeah, but we can join you. Call us when you go down. There are three restaurants. The main one is great. They even have a piano player. Have you called Tom?" Amanda asked.

"We've just arrived. I'm going to call as soon as we get to our room." Faith took the keys to the room and they went to the elevator.

Inside the elevator, Tina leaned against the wall. "After weeks of washing our clothes in sinks and tubs, it's going to feel great getting them really clean in a washing machine. I'm going to put out all my clothes except what I'm wearing tonight and my pajamas as soon as we get to our room. Tomorrow we can trade out tonight's wear," Tina said.

"Sounds like a plan," Faith said.

While Tina showered, Faith called Tom.

Tom answered on the first ring.

"It's me. Remember me," Faith said.

"Barely. It's so good to hear your voice."

Faith poured her heart out making sure not to reveal too many hardships.

Tom listened intently, "Your voice sounds much better than it did the last time we talked. I've been really worried about you and Amanda."

"We're getting into the routine of things and I'm dealing with things much better," Faith said.

When Faith hung up the phone, the words "I love and miss you," seemed to have so much more meaning than they had in the past.

While Faith showered, Tina called home.

After Faith dressed and came out of the bathroom she noticed that Tina looked more relaxed than she had on the trip so far.

Faith called Amanda's room and upon leaving their room to head for the restaurant, they placed the hotel's laundry bag with all their dirty clothes outside the door.

Sitting in a modern hotel restaurant Faith was surprised that her emotions were so mixed over staying in this modern hotel. She was grateful for the ability to shop, and get reorganized. Yet, she had a nagging feeling, *I feel like I'm cheating, taking this break.*

Tina laughed, "You can tell we are in civilization. Look at the menu. We can get a Rueben or hamburger. There's even spaghetti. And I bet its American style, too."

Faith smiled. She was about to express how unsettling staying in the hotel was to her. But before she spoke she saw Amanda and Rachael enter the restaurant. The looks on their faces expressed that were happy to be off the trail for a break. Seeing their happy faces, she accepted their were benefits to taking a break in a modern hotel.

That evening the four enjoyed a relaxing evening. The mishaps of the trip to date became topics of humor, and when Faith climbed into a queen size, firm bed, in an air-conditioned room with no entertainment outside their room to keep her awake; she slept soundly.

The following morning, the morning sun entered their room.

Faith pushed a button by her bed and watched the blackout curtain automatically drop over the windows. She wasn't ready to get up. She felt like she could sleep the day away. Just for fun, she hit the button again and watched it retract into the ceiling. Again, she pushed the button. This time, she let the curtain remain in its position blocking the sun from entering the room. She felt like she was in heaven. It was going to be so hard to get back on the road. Cuddled up in bed, Faith reviewed the last few days in her mind. She knew she'd never be able to describe what they'd been through or what an 18% grade climb looks like. She never imagined she would climb sheer cliffs using tree branches as ropes to get up the sides of those cliffs. And there would be no way to relay the kindness people in villages and on farms have shown them along the way.

Later that day, all seven met to tour the Basilica of Begona. A wedding was in progress. They moved quietly through the basilica not wanting to disturb the couple and their guests. Then, it was on to the Guggenheim museum.

Outside the museum, Faith stopped a young woman and asked if she would take a picture of the group standing in front of *The Cat* sculpture completely draped in live colorful flowers. For the first time on the trip, everyone seemed in good spirits.

"Faith, I hear you and Tina got a massage today. How was it?" Honey asked.

"It was fabulous," Faith replied.

Amanda took Rachael's arm "We're getting massages before dinner. We're off to see the Bascilica de Bagone now. There's a club within walking distance. Later this evening we were thinking of checking it out. Anyone want to join us?"

"I didn't think I was going to make it yesterday, but I'm feeling pretty good. I'm game," Tina answered.

"This may be the only time we'll have a chance to sleep in after a night out, I'll go," Faith answered.

"Me too," Honey answered.

"I'll see how I feel after dinner. Leave word at the front desk where we can find you. I might join you," Jocelyn said.

"The idea of a massage sounded good. I'm going to see if I can schedule one. See you later," Honey announced as she left the group.

Honey was able to schedule a massage two hours after the group separated. To her surprise she had difficulty relaxing. Thoughts kept churning in her mind. Things seemed to be going well with the group. She hoped it would it would last.

"You sure are tight. Can I ask you a question?" the masseuse asked.

"Sure," Honey answered, happy for the distraction.

"Not too many pilgrims come and stay at the Sheraton, but the pilgrims I do see have similar problems. Most have blistered feet and tell me how hard the hike is. So, why are you doing it?"

Honey couldn't share why she was on this pilgrimage. She searched her mind for other reasons, and answered, "They do it to find spiritual inner peace."

"And you, why are you?"

Honey took a breath. She searched her mind for an appropriate answer. Her first thought was to say, 'to make my man happy.' Instead, she answered with a smile in her voice, "To get back my girlish figure."

Later that evening, all seven gathered to participate in an evening of fun and frolic. Early in the evening conversation remained pleasant. Honey had hopes for some sort of reconciliation between Tina and Jocelyn. Her hope was short lived. Out of the blue, Jocelyn said, "So, Tina, are you going to take a cab out of the city?"

Faith shook her head in disgust. "Jocelyn, I don't know why you feel the need to antagonize Tina, but I wish you would stop."

"It was a simple question," Jocelyn replied.

Faith heard the words of St. Francis echo in her mind, *Lord, make me an instrument of your peace.* Faith took a deep breath and said, "Jocelyn you've said it before. This is your trip and you don't need to be worrying about others."

Jocelyn shrugged her shoulders, stood, and walked away.

12

BILBAO TO PORTUGALETE

After searching two hours for the yellow arrow which would direct them out of town, Faith was pleased to see Tina's spirits were still good. But when they came to the marker and Faith looked at an upward spiraling set of steps, she realized she'd mistakenly told Tina today was supposed to be relatively flat and easy. Yet, there they were climbing steps right off the get-go. She looked at Tina. She couldn't believe her eyes. She wasn't complaining.

When the ground leveled off, they observed a middle-aged woman wearing a wide-brimmed straw-hat, a loose-fitting, long-sleeved blouse, and skirt. She was feeding the chickens while her husband cut corn in a nearby field. The road that ran alongside the farm had deep ruts from the passing oxcarts.

Faith waved at the couple as they passed by. *This is so amazing. I hope Amanda and Rachael are having a good time. They must be miles ahead of us by now. There will be little chance of catching up to them now.*

Several miles ahead of Faith and Tina; Jocelyn, Ada, and Honey found a tapas bar open. Refreshed and grateful for the short lunch stop, they found the next hours passed easier than anticipated. They came to a concrete bridge bordered on both sides with park benches for the convenience of walkers or riders to rest or view the stream below. It was wide enough for people to walk without getting in the way of cyclists.

At a high trail point that forked to the right, the yellow arrow pointed downward directing travelers to continue along the concrete walkway. The other direction led up a dirt path high into the hills. Honey was grateful the path sloped downward, although she felt there was something disconcerting about it. She noticed the stone walls were very tall. Dense foliage covered the walls. Little light found its way to the path. It looked dark and foreboding.

As they turned to head down into the ravine, an older gentleman wearing a worn suit jacket and beret rose from a park bench and quickly approached. He spoke Spanish and waved his arms. Using the best sign language he could muster he attempted to direct the women away from the path that lead down into the ravine. He pointed frantically directing them toward the dirt path that would take them up and around.

"Can you make out what he is saying?" Ada asked.

"My Spanish isn't great, but I believe he is trying to tell us that there are gypsies down there," Honey said.

"So what? They won't bother us. I'm sure he's just an old crazy man. I'm not listening to this nonsense. We've got to get going. It's getting late. Let's go," Jocelyn said.

Honey watched the old man. He shrugged his shoulders and shook his head as they walked away.

After some time they came to an area, thick with trees. Suddenly, high-pitched voices emanated from the shadows. Gypsies came out from behind a stone wall, and surrounded them. Women in flowing skirts lifted them high in the air revealing their privates. Some opened their blouses to reveal their breasts, as their bodies gyrated obscenely. Two men joined them and laughed loudly while holding their hands over their privates acting out humping gestures. The gypsies circled and followed them all the way to the edge of the ravine, but did not touch them, and laughed hysterically as the three inched their way out of the ravine.

As soon as Honey knew they were out of ear shot, she yelled, "Jocelyn, we're just lucky they didn't rob us or worse. That was a nauseating experience. Your stubbornness and pushiness is going to get us into trouble."

Honey noticed Ada's facial expression revealed fear and disgust.

"Ada, why don't you speak up? I can see you're upset, too."

"Nothing I say will change anything," Ada answered in a solemn, distant tone.

Jocelyn's face turned red. "Honey if you don't like it, you can go it on your own. I've walked alone many times and I don't need this flack. We could have run into them on the other trail just as easily."

"You may be right, and I'm sure, with your attitude, you won't wait to see if the other girls make it out okay."

"You're right about that. If you want to wait, be my quest."

Ada reached and held Honey's arm. "There would be nothing to be gained by waiting or going back. Let's just hope they take that old man's advice."

Honey held her tongue. She knew Ada was right. Besides, the gypsies might scare Amanda and Rachael. This could be just the ticket she was looking for.

Amanda and Rachael came to the same crossroads the others had.

The older gentleman watched as the girls examined the yellow arrow. *"Bon Camino?"* he asked.

"Si," Rachael answered with a broad smile.

The man explained what he had to the others. Rachael thanked him, but before they started up the hill, Amanda asked, "Rachael, do you think Mom and Tina will know enough to come this way?"

"Only if someone is here to tell them, and we can't count on that."

"I guess we should take a break and wait on them. I've got some bread and cheese. Wish I had some wine to go with it," Amanda said.

They waited two hours before Faith and Tina arrived at the crossroads.

Surprised to see Amanda and Rachael, Tina asked. "What are you doing here? I expected you'd be at the hotel by now."

"We decided to wait. There are gypsies down in the ravine. We were told by a villager that we should follow a different path." Amanda pointed to a path on the mountainside, "That one. We didn't want you to take the wrong road," Amanda said.

"We really appreciate your waiting, but you're going to be more tired tonight than ever. Sitting waiting on us must have driven you nuts," Faith said.

"It wasn't so bad. It was fun talking to passersby," Rachael said.

After a short climb, the walk took them through a beautiful countryside dotted with small, yellow wildflowers where butterflies danced all around them. Fascinated by the sights and an endless parade of creatures, the four enjoyed each other's company. They shared funny stories, and, at times walked in silence looking out to a turquoise ocean, graced above by big, white, fluffy clouds. In the distance, they could see villages nestled along the seashore.

"One of those villages is our destination, and I don't care if I have to eat extra late, but I'm going to take the time to put my feet into that ocean water. They're killing me, and the water looks so inviting," Faith said.

"That sounds good to me," Rachael said.

Amanda giggled, "And to me, too."

"When we get there, I'm heading to the room. I don't have it in me to walk another step. I'll rest until dinner," Tina said.

At the hotel, Faith, Amanda, and Rachael dropped their bags in their rooms then went directly to the shore. With rolled-up pant legs and bare feet, they ran into the water, and were soon totally drenched and enjoying the swim. Out of the water, clothes clung heavily on their bodies. Happy as young children, they dropped onto the sand.

Seeing Amanda relaxed, Faith asked, "Are you enjoying the trip?"

"I'm having a blast," Amanda said. "I could do without the nonsense that goes on between Tina and Jocelyn, and some of the pain in my feet, but otherwise, I love Spain and the people. Rachael is enjoying the trip, too."

"Glad to hear it," Faith said.

"And how about you and Tina, how are you doing?" Amanda asked.

"At first, I had my doubts, with Tina finding the trip so difficult. But now that she's getting into the groove, I am finding the trip more enjoyable. Except, I wish you and I could spend more time together."

"Well, we're together, now," Amanda said.

Faith reached out and gently touched her daughter's hand. "Yes, we are."

Rachael walked to them and held her soaked pant legs away from her body, "This feels gross. I'm ready to get cleaned up. How about you two?"

Faith and Amanda answered in unison, "Ready."

13

PORTUGALETE TO LAREDO

The last two days had taken a toll on Honey's nerves. She couldn't stop worrying about how to get into Amanda's suitcase to get rid of her allergy medicine. It hadn't helped that the terrain from Portugalete through Castro Urdiales and on to Laredo had them zigzagging up and over hills and traversing sheer cliffs, and Jocelyn's pushing had only added to the tension.

Now, following a good night's sleep, Honey stood on Main Street and watched professional cyclists race by. She wished she could relax, but found she was too agitated over the Amanda situation.

When she saw Amanda and Rachael cross the street to join her, Honey felt her heart beating faster. Tomorrow after dinner she would go to their room and ask Amanda for a couple of her allergy pills. While pretending to take a couple of pills, she'd take the bottle, hid it, and take it with her.

Rachael smiled, "Don't you love the bright colors on those racers' outfits? And their cute little butts?"

"You're making me blush," Honey said.

Rachael smiled, "Yeah, sure. Don't you love this town? Our hotel is so adorable. There probably aren't more than 12 rooms in our hotel."

"Yes, it's delightful. I had a snack on the patio. The garden area is charming. No matter what the order, they bring homemade cheese and olives that are out of this world. So, what are you girls up to today?" Honey asked.

"Not much. We might take a walk along the beach. Only the thought of walking on a day off just doesn't sound right. We haven't even figured out dinner yet. Want us to call you when we figure it out?" Rachael asked.

Honey, pleased with the offer, answered, "Sounds like a possibility. I'll check in with you later this afternoon."

"See you later," Amanda said.

Honey returned to the hotel, leaving the girls to their happy exploits. In the hotel courtyard, she found Tina lounging in a chair with steno pad and pen in hand. "Hi. Tina, this place is great, don't you think?"

"You couldn't ask for a better day. The temperature is perfect, not a drop of rain, and comfortable arrangements," Tina answered.

"I ran into Amanda and Rachael. They were watching a bicycle race. Pretty interesting. It went right through town."

"I know. Before I came down, I watched out my room's window as they passed our hotel. Some hot-looking boys. I can see why they're staying where the action is," Tina said.

"Am I intruding?" Honey asked.

"Not at all. I simply need to write in my diary as soon as possible. If I wait too long, I forget what's happened."

"Same for me. Is it too early for a glass of wine? I'm buying," Honey said.

"Not for me. Its afternoon and a glass of wine will probably help relax me. I plan to take a long nap after I get my diary caught up."

"Great. I'll go inside and get a couple of tapas, too."

When Honey returned, Tina put away her diary.

"Our order should be out shortly. With things being what they are, we haven't had much time to talk. I can't believe two weeks have passed. The days seem to go by slowly and yet, here we are," Honey said.

"I could have gone home the first two days, but now, I'm doing okay."

Honey got comfy in a chair. "You're doing great."

"I'm making progress. Although I'm sure Jocelyn and Ada wouldn't agree. As it turns out, I'm finding the pilgrimage is helping me in ways I hadn't thought of previously. It's helping me get over my anger. I didn't realize how angry I was over my husband's illness," Tina said.

"Look, I'm not sure what's wrong with Jocelyn, but this pilgrimage is tough for all of us. The only difference is the rest of us started in better shape," Honey said.

"Why did you decide to go on the pilgrimage?" Tina asked.

Honey's breathing became erratic. She had rehearsed several answers, knowing this question would certainly arise. She searched her mind for an appropriate one, and then said, "I always wanted to see Spain, and I like challenges. When Jocelyn mentioned the trip, it sounded like a great idea. Years ago, I used to hike often in the mountains of North Carolina, Wyoming, and Colorado."

Over the next hour, Honey gathered little bits and pieces of information about Tina, Amanda, and Faith. She purposely avoided mentioning Amanda's father's murder. She hoped Tina would bring the subject up but to Honey's regret; Tina never did.

"This has been fun, but I'm going to call it. I'm ready for my nap. It sounds like everyone is eating here at the hotel this evening. Guess I'll see you later," Tina said.

When Honey went to her room, Ada was asleep. Honey kicked off her shoes, sat on her bed, and pulled a pillow from under the covers. She propped the pillow behind her back, got comfortable, took out her journal, and wrote:

> It has been days since I reflected on my travels. I am anxious to get this job finished and behind me. I have never harmed someone before, much less killed someone. I know Faith needs to suffer for the hurt she has caused Ivan; but as I travel with Amanda, I'm finding it harder to think about taking her life. I've made contact with the enemy, but befriending the enemy before the slaughter is affecting me more than I had anticipated. I wish I could talk to Ivan. His voice would give me strength. Tomorrow, my plan will go into effect, and Ivan's revenge will be secure. Faith will suffer at her daughter's loss. This shall be proper payment for Ivan's imprisonment. I need to stay strong.

Honey closed her journal, stretched out on the bed, and closed her eyes.

An hour later, Ada awoke and said, "Boy, were you having some harsh dreams. You've been tossing and turning, and talking in your sleep.

Honey acted nonchalant as she asked, "Really? What did I say?"

"I have no idea, nothing that made any sense. Hey, after all the near misses we've had over the last few days, you're probably just a little frazzled. I know I am. Did you see the cycling today?"

"Yeah. I've always wondered what a peloton would look like up close and personal. They were moving so fast, if you blinked, you'd miss them," Honey said.

"And so close, too. It looked scary to me. By the way, Jocelyn plans to eat here in the hotel. I think the others will do the same. Dinner is set for 8:00 p.m.," Ada said.

"Sounds good."

Later at supper, Honey sat with Jocelyn and Ada, not wanting to bring attention to the fact she was cozying up to Amanda.

After a wonderful dinner, Honey went to her room. In bed, she tossed and turned. She couldn't quiet her thoughts. Sleep came slowly.

14

LAREDO TO NOJA

While Honey walked she had trouble deciphering whether her fatigue came from the thought of tackling another long day's walk, the threatening gray skies, or from worry over something going wrong with her plan to poison Amanda.

The route from Laredo to Noja followed the coastline, weaving in and out of villages. At times, the trail took the three groups onto old country roads. The rain fell, and the wind blew. On the country roads their feet stuck in mud, and slipped over slick rocks. Other times, the route took them on paved roads with heavy traffic. The cars and trucks drove so fast and close that Honey held onto her poncho for fear it would catch on a side-view mirror. That was until she realized that most cars already had their mirrors broken off.

Water from passing cars splashed onto Honey's poncho, boots, and face. In front of her she watched

Ada's and Jocelyn's ponchos flap in the wind. The site conjured up thoughts of monks hiking across Spain, pushing their way into the wind on a rainy day.

As the day unfolded, the sun tried to come out, but gray clouds continued to win. The humidity rose and sweat poured down Honey's body. She felt uncomfortably trapped inside her blue poncho.

At the top of a hill, Honey stopped and called out to Ada, "I'm going to stop for a minute. I need to take off this poncho. I feel like I'm in a sauna." Ada and Jocelyn stopped and removed their ponchos as well.

"I feel human again," Honey said.

Ada and Jocelyn nodded in agreement.

While the breeze cooled her body, Honey delighted in the view. The hillside was dotted with small villages. In the far distance the sea crashed against the rocks along the shore. In some ways she was feeling bad about killing Amanda. The group probably wouldn't finish the trip. Yet, the more she thought about, she had suspicions that Jocelyn would continue onward. Once Honey got a message to Ivan that Amanda was dead, he wouldn't care if she took a couple of extra weeks in Spain before heading home.

After 10 hours of hiking, Honey, Jocelyn, and Ada reached the outskirts of Noja. None of their maps or hotel reservation papers gave a clue where they would find their accommodations. They followed one person's directions after another's. None took them to their hotel, and twice they came back to a familiar spot.

After adding another hour to the day, with no encouragement they would find their hotel, they hailed a cab. After giving him the address, the cab driver smiled, and in poor, but understandable English said, "Wonderful place. My cousin works there."

"Honey gave him an approving glance. "That's great."

To her surprise, on their way to the hotel, in a very defensive tone, Jocelyn said, "Look, tomorrow is supposed to be longer and much tougher than today. It's late, so we will need to replenish our supplies the first chance we get."

Ada and Honey nodded acknowledging Jocelyn's statement.

After they checked into the hotel, Honey went to the hotel's kitchen concerned that the others might get to the hotel too late or too tired for supper. She needed to keep an eye on Amanda. If they left the hotel, it would be much harder for her to keep track of there movements. She explained their dilemma to the cook, and asked, "Could you put some food aside for my companions, in case they get here after the restaurant has closed?"

Kind and accommodating, the cook told Honey he would make sure soup, fresh bread and cheese would be waiting, no matter how late they arrived.

An hour later, Honey checked in at the front desk. The clerk informed her that two young girls had arrived, and were in their rooms. She took in a deep breath content that her biggest worry was out of the way. Amanda had arrived.

Another hour passed by before Faith and Tina arrived. The rest of the group had already eaten. Jocelyn and Ada had called it a night.

Back in her room, Honey waited a respectable amount of time then, made an excuse to go out for water. She found Amanda and Rachael still up, snacking on cheese and crackers in the lobby.

"Amanda, I gather your mom and Tina made it in okay." Honey said.

"Yep. Thanks for arranging to have the cook save some dinner for them. They're in the restaurant."

"Great. I won't bother them. Tell them I'll see them in the morning."

Honey picked up her water and returned to her room. Although exhausted, she wrote in her journal until she believed Amanda and Rachael were settled in their room.

Convinced enough time had passed, Honey climbed out of bed. She couldn't tell whether Ada was asleep. "Ada, are you asleep?"

"Not yet. Is something wrong?" Ada asked.

"No. I asked Amanda to pick up something for me. I should get it this evening, in case I miss her in the morning or forget again."

"You better take the key to the room. I'll probably be asleep by the time you get back," Ada said.

"Sure thing."

Honey knocked on Amanda's door, "Who is it?" Rachael asked.

"Honey."

"The door is locked. Hold on, I'll get it."

When Honey entered the room, she could see that the girls had already settled into bed.

"Anything wrong?" Rachael asked.

"No. With all the confusion this evening, I forgot to ask Amanda if she had a chance to get that anti-inflammatory for me yesterday. I forgot all about it, but as soon as I went to bed, my back stiffened and reminded me."

"Sure. I'm sorry. I forgot, too. I'll get it," Amanda said.

Quickly, Honey said, "Don't get up. I'll get it. Just tell me where it is."

"It's in my suitcase in my medicine bag, the small pink bag."

Honey turned the bag so the girls couldn't see her remove Amanda's medicine.

Amanda noticed Honey was having difficulty in finding her package, and asked, "Need some help?"

Honey's voice stuttered, "No, no, thanks. I've found it."

Controlling her jittering hand, Honey closed the suitcase, and thanked Amanda. After Honey was outside the room, she closed her eyes, and sighed deeply. It had been a long day. Now, all that was left was to fix sandwiches in the morning.

15

NOJA TO SANTANDER (THE PLAN)

Purposely waking before the others, Honey stood at her open hotel window. Darkness covered the landscape. She inhaled the fresh scent of the previous night's cleansing rain. Up and out of bed early, she prepared sandwiches unobserved. She gingerly opened the bag of freshly baked bread, to prevent waking Ada. She pulled the bread out and cut it into enough thick slices to make seven sandwiches. She prepared a sandwich for herself and put it aside. She couldn't take any chances that Amanda might pick up someone else's sandwich, so prepared each sandwich in the same manner. She took the small plastic bag of crushed shrimp she had brought back to her room, and mixed it into the jar of chunky, spiced orange marmalade. She took a taste, and didn't detect any difference. She finished preparing the peanut butter and marmalade sandwiches and placed them into baggies, then set them into a larger bag. She smiled with the realization that today Amanda would die and Ivan would be avenged.

When Honey entered the breakfast area a waiter greeted her then asked, "Would you like cappuccino, tea, or regular coffee?"

"Cappuccino, please."

While Honey drank her coffee, she felt her heart pounding rapidly. *Stop worrying. They'll be down soon. Amanda loves peanut butter sandwiches. She'll eat it for lunch without giving it a second thought.*

Tina and Faith were the first to join Honey for breakfast.

Faith smiled at Honey, "Looks like someone is ready to get an early start."

"A woodpecker pounding on the wall woke me and I couldn't get back to sleep." Honey lied.

Honey waited until the entire group was present then, picked up the bag that held the sandwiches, and announced, "I made peanut butter and marmalade sandwiches for everyone. I couldn't resist. I bought fresh bread last night, and figured an extra sandwich couldn't hurt. Finding food today could be difficult."

"What a great idea! I know I'll be happy to have something extra to eat in my bag," Tina said.

Honey set the sandwiches on a table, and each member of the group picked up one up as they left the restaurant. Jocelyn went to the doorway. "Honey, we're ready to go."

Honey noticed the wind tugged at the awnings of the hotel. At the outskirts of town when they returned to the mountain landscape the morning wind set off a low whistle in the trees. They trudged along muddy roads through farmlands most of the morning.

Around 11:00 a.m. they came to a church. Ada suggested they stop to rest, so they sat on a nearby stone wall. Ada and Jocelyn pulled out the sandwiches Honey had made for them. Honey took out her sandwich, and as she ate, she watched Ada and Jocelyn for any signs that they thought their sandwiches tasted funny. They seemed to be enjoying their sandwiches, and made no comment as to their tasting oddly.

While the three rested, Honey noticed a car drive up to the church and as an elderly couple got out, a nun stepped out of the church, walked toward the couple, and assisted them to the church entrance. The nun left the couple inside the church, stepped out again, and walked over to where Honey and the others were sitting. She invited them to Mass, lifted their packs off the ground, and directed them to follow her into the chapel.

Honey, Jocelyn, and Ada all tried their best to dissuade the nun. They pointed to their dirty clothes, implying it would be too embarrassing for them to go inside. The nun was determined. She took their backpacks to a safe-room. After she closed and locked the door, she gestured that the packs would be secure. This left them little choice except to attend Mass. The three sat on a bench close to the back while parishioners straggled in over the next half hour.

Honey studied the workmanship of this small chapel. She admired a monstrous pipe organ off to one side of the altar as the sun shown through the stained glass windows accentuating gold ornate carvings.

Twelve monks assembled near the pipe organ. Their voices and the organ joined as one. The sound of their chanting was mesmerizing.

Honey shivered. Her head felt heavy. Chills traveled up and down her spine, and her eyes watered. She remembered days in her youth when she and her family attended Mass. That was before her mother's passing, and her father's physical abuse began. She felt God had abandoned her. She had no fear of hell. She had lived there all her life. The only peace, the only comfort she'd found was with Ivan.

Honey saw Jocelyn and Ada look her way. She couldn't let them see any emotions. She'd always managed to keep her feelings in check.

As the monk's voices filled the chapel, Honey wanted to get up and run out, but she sat still as a statue. Her thoughts drifted. She envisioned Amanda taking her last breath. Suddenly fear, followed by doubt, surged through her body. *I've killed her. The deed is done.*

16

NOJA TO SANTANDER (THE VISION)

Rachael and Amanda had begun their day walking with Tina and Faith. Faith suspected the heavy downpour of rain was responsible for their starting out at such a slow pace. However, whatever the reason, Faith appreciated the extra time spent with her daughter. When the sun came out, Faith's suspicions about the girl's rate of speed were confirmed as their pace increased.

Observing the change, Faith said, "Tina and I are going to stop and rest. You girls go ahead. We'll catch up with you later."

"If we find anything open along the way, we'll probably stop. We might see you sooner than later," Rachel said.

"Nice thought girls, but I suspect it will be later."

Within minutes, the girls were over the ridge.

"I wonder where Jocelyn and her crew are. They probably made it to that village in time for lunch," Tina said.

"It doesn't matter how far they've gotten. All that matters is we're here and that we're making progress. You've said it yourself: This isn't a race, it's a pilgrimage."

"Faith, you don't have to go so slow. Go ahead at your own speed. You can wait for me at the next turn."

"I'll go a little ways ahead, and scope it out."

The air had cooled following the rain. Faith pushed up the hill allowing her frustrations to fade away under the spell of wildflowers, wind, and overhead clouds. She came to the top of the ridge. It looked like a good place to stop and wait, and a great place to say a few Sunday morning prayers. She couldn't find a better church anywhere.

In the middle of a prayer, she felt as if she had risen above her body. An angel appeared, and in her dream state, she saw a vision of Amanda lying on the ground. Her eyes flashed open. *Amanda's in trouble. I need to get to her.*

She looked down the hill. Tina was close to the top. Not far behind Tina she saw an unusual sight. Coming up the path was a man with a cart with wooden wheels being pulled by a donkey. She couldn't get to Amanda walking with Tina at their pace. She decided to ask the man for help. She knew it was crazy, but she felt she needed to get to her daughter soon.

Faith ran down the hill to Tina, "Wait here. I'll be right back. Amanda is in trouble. I've got to get to her."

To Faith's surprise, Tina answered, "I know. I felt it, too. You go ahead without me. I can make it the rest of the way on my own."

"Don't worry, I'll be right back, hopefully with help," Faith called back as she continued down the mountain to the man and his donkey cart.

The driver halted upon seeing Faith running toward him.

When Faith reached the cart, in her best Spanish, she explained the problem. To Faith, it seemed as if he understood. He gestured for her to climb into the back of the wagon. When they made their way to Tina, the man called out to his burro to stop. He climbed off his seat, and smiled at Tina before helping her onto the seat next to where he sat. Faith thought, *This is strange. He's flirting with her.*

After the driver was seated, he signaled his faithful burro to get a move on.

As the cart moved rapidly down the path, bouncing over rocks, Faith watched the man's cargo of fresh fruits and vegetables spring into the air and drop back into their crates. In between bounces, she noticed Tina and the kindly gentleman exchange friendly glances.

17

NOJA TO SANTANDER (SAFE)

Amanda had seen an inviting plot of grass under an even more tempting shade tree.

As Amanda and Rachael sat under the tree, they ate while observing a small village far off in the distance.

They each pulled out a bottle of water from their packs along with Honey's sandwich, an orange, and a small bag of jelly beans. They ate and drank while enjoying the fresh mountain breeze and the splendor of the countryside's expanse that spread out in front of them.

When they finished their snacks, they stretched out on the ground to rest before resuming their hike.

For a moment Amanda felt like she was in paradise. That was until her face, hands and feet began to itch. She had trouble swallowing. Panic rang through her voice, "Rachael, something's wrong. I'm having an attack."

Rachael quickly went into action. She pulled out Amanda's medicine bag. She couldn't find her tablets. Amanda's face continued to redden, and her breathing became more strained.

Rachael pulled out a washcloth she carried in her backpack, and drenched it with water. She placed it on Amanda's forehead.

Amanda's eyes filled with tears. She struggled, gasping for air.

Rachael feared the worse. "Amanda, can you slow down your breathing? Try to take shallower breaths."

Rachael used her backpack as a pillow for Amanda to rest her head on. Lying still on her back, Amanda's breathing became less erratic, but Rachael's fears were not relieved. Amanda's swelling face seemed to double in size. Rachael kept wetting the washcloth for Amanda's forehead, while thinking, *If I leave her to get help, I may not get back to her in time. I don't want to leave her, but what else can I do?*

Rachael took her jacket out of her backpack and put it over Amanda's chest and wrapped it close in around her shoulders, then, softly she touched Amanda's shoulder. "I need to get help. But, you've got to promise to remain still until I get back. Promise?"

Amanda took her hand, squeezed it, and nodded.

Trembling, Rachael stood to leave. *I'm sure I'll find help.* Then, in the distance, Rachael saw what appeared to be a wagon pulled by a donkey. *Whoever is driving that cart might live close by, or at least, may know someone who lives close by who can help.*

Rachael took off down the hill while calling back to Amanda, "Hang in there. Help is on the way."

As she neared the wagon, she shook her head in disbelief. *Is that Tina on that wagon?*

When she reached the wagon, she saw Tina sitting next to the driver. Then, Faith popped her head up from the back of the cart. "Rachael, where's Amanda? What's happened?"

Frantically, Rachael said, "She's had another attack. I couldn't find her medicine. She needs to get to a doctor!" In Spanish, she told the driver, "My friend is at the ridge under that tree. She's in trouble."

Rachael ran back to Amanda. Faith jumped off the wagon and ran with her. The burro followed his master's orders pulling the wagon quickly down the graveled dirt path.

As soon as Amanda was in Faith's sight, out of breath, she called out, "Amanda, I'm here."

Amanda didn't answer. She was unconscious. Faith dropped to the ground, leaned in to check her daughter's breathing. It was present, but faint.

Rachael saw the panicked look on Faith's face as she pulled an EpiPen from her pack. "How long has she been unconscious?"

"At most, five minutes. She was conscious when I left to go to you," Rachael answered.

Faith gave Amanda a shot of epinephrine, held her daughter, and they all waited. Within minutes Amanda's color started to return to normal, but she was still very weak. The driver helped Amanda into the back of the cart, and graciously offered to take her to the next town, to a friend's home.

The driver went slowly while Faith, Tina, and Rachael walked behind the donkey cart. Faith could see Amanda's face. Amanda kept waving and smiling, attempting to show she was okay. When they arrived at the farmhouse, a woman with big friendly brown eyes greeted them. The driver introduced his sister to the group, and explained the situation. She quickly offered them food and drinks and her couch for Amanda to rest on. They ate while Amanda rested. However, within the hour, Amanda announced that she was well enough to make the rest of the day's journey.

"Amanda, I know you could make it, but if I can hire the driver to take you to the hotel; I would feel better," Faith said.

The driver understood her English, and offered to take Amanda. However, he refused to take payment for the service.

Rachael gave the driver the name of the hotel where they were staying, and Amanda agreed to go with him.

Tina quickly volunteered her services. "I'll go with Amanda."

The driver smiled, looking pleased with the idea of Tina continuing on with him.

"Guess that leaves us," Rachael said.

Faith looked at Rachael, "Are you sure you don't want to hitch a ride?"

"I'd rather not. The ways things are going, you never know what could happen to prevent a day's walk."

"Well if you're game, so am I," Faith said.

Faith and Rachael waved good-bye and watched the cart travel down the path.

The terrain was difficult, but following Amanda's close call, Faith had little more on her mind than gratitude for having gotten to her daughter in time. God had sent her a message that Amanda was in trouble, then an angel. She smiled thinking he had been a funny angel with a burro, but an angel just the same.

18

SANTANDER

At the end of a long day, under heavy black clouds, Honey, Jocelyn, and Ada came to a gentle slope in the path. Thunder rolled and rumbled, threateningly over the ridges and back through the hollows. The sea mist and ocean breeze gave the women hope they were close to their night's destination. Tile roofs speckled the hillside that lined the shoreline of Santander. Still two miles out from the city, the roar of the ocean could be heard as it hit the coastal rocks.

The path leveled out into a trail of compacted dirt. Honey marveled at the countryside as the soft green grass bowed under the power of the wind. Amanda was dead. She should have felt good, but she didn't.

Are you okay?" Ada asked.

"Just tired.'

Honey noticed Ada's face looked drained as she reported. "I'm not doing well. Something has gotten my stomach churning, and I've got a splitting headache. Jocelyn isn't feeling great either. It feels like food poisoning,"

Listening to Ada, Honey realized Jocelyn had been stopping more than usual to rest.

"Ada, I'm sorry to hear you're not feeling well. We should reach our hotel soon. I'll catch up to Jocelyn, and see how she's doing."

"That would be good. I believe Jocelyn thinks we're all mad at her. She's been awfully defensive," Ada said.

"We're all tired."

Before Honey left Ada to join Jocelyn, she had a terrible thought, *What if someone figures out it was my sandwiches that made everyone sick?* She needed to make sure no traces of the sandwiches remained.

"You know, I've had a headache, and my stomach has been a little queasy, too. Maybe, we should eat something. That might help settle our stomachs," Honey said.

"I've consumed everything in my pack," Ada said.

Honey pulled some crackers from her backpack. "Here, eat a couple of these. They might help."

"Thanks."

Relieved that at least one sandwich had been eliminated, Honey joined Jocelyn. "Ada and I aren't feeling too good. How are you doing?"

"I'm not my perky self," Jocelyn answered.

"Do you have anything to eat in your pack? Eating might help to settle your stomach," Honey suggested.

"All I have is an apple. And I don't want to eat anything right now."

Great, Honey thought, *She isn't connecting the sandwich to her problem either.*

Shortly thereafter, Honey, Ada, and Jocelyn regrouped, and made their way to the first pharmacy they came to. They purchased medicine for their upset stomachs and continued to their hotel. On the way they came to a life-size statue of Don Quixote.

"A good friend of mine collects Don Quixote memorabilia. I hope we can find a replica of this statue in one of the shops before we leave town. Can we stop and get a Coke? I better take this medicine. I'm feeling worse," Ada said.

Honey tried to catch Jocelyn to let her know that they were stopping, but she was moving so fast she decided to let her go.

"It looks like Jocelyn is on a mission to get the hotel," Honey said.

A few blocks from where they were standing, Ada saw a tapas bar, "Can we stop at that tapas bar? A soda might help to settle my stomach."

"Sure."

After a short break, Honey and Ada left for the hotel. They discovered their luggage sitting unattended in the middle of the sidewalk at the top of six-tiered sets of stairs. All bags were there, except for Jocelyn's. Honey presumed she had taken it with her.

Ada and Honey picked up their and slowly made their way down the steps. When they reached the hotel, they found the registry book on a desk sitting in the middle of what appeared to be a communal living room. The keys to assigned rooms lay on the desk next to the sign-in book where each of their names had been written in next to a room number. Their rooms were three levels up, and the hotel did not have an elevator.

"Ada, I'll take care of getting the bags to our room. You go on up. I'll be there in a minute." Next to the register was a note left by Jocelyn.

> I picked up some chicken soup on my way here.
> I'm skipping dinner, and will see you in the morning.
> I'll be in the lobby at 7:30 a.m.

Honey's neck and shoulders tightened as she read Jocelyn's note. When she got their bags into the room, she could hear Ada in the bathroom throwing up. Honey tried to talk to her, but Ada couldn't say anything, except. "Let me be. I'll be okay."

Honey needed to get out of the room. Soup sounded good.

She went to the bathroom door. "Ada, soup might help to settle our stomachs. I'm going out and get us a couple of bowls. Don't worry about having to answer the door when I return. I've got a key."

Downstairs, Honey looked for the custodian of the house. She scoped the area for some signs of life. Finding no one in sight, figuring there was nothing more she could do, she went out for soup.

After climbing the three blocks of worn, irregularly shaped concrete steps, Honey traveled two more blocks before she found a restaurant. After ordering their soup, she ordered and drank two glasses of wine while waiting for them to package up the soup. Before leaving she bought a bottle of wine to take back to their room.

When she returned to her room with the soup, she found Ada's condition had not improved. She poured a glass of wine, and picked up a book to read while waiting for the report of Amanda's death to reach the hotel.

Honey waited in her room until 8:30 p.m. then disconcerted over no news arriving of Amanda's death, she went to the lounge area. She found the hotel's custodian serving tea, and asked, "Have my friends arrived? Their room numbers are 32 and 34?"

"Yes. Would you like me to take a message to their rooms?"

His answer took her by surprise. His words seemed to be coming from a faraway place. Honey became light-headed. Her knees buckled. After she regained her composure, she asked. "How many arrived?"

"I checked in four. Two arrived about an hour earlier than the others."

Honey felt perspiration form at her temples. She stepped out of the lounge area into the street to cool down. *Amanda must not have eaten her sandwich. What am I going to do now?*

Frustrated, Honey went to the outdoor café located next to their hotel and ordered another glass of wine. She couldn't believe that Amanda hadn't eaten her sandwich, and that her plan had again backfired.

Sipping her wine she contemplated her next approach to kill Amanda she was shocked and jumped in her seat when she heard Faith's voice behind her. "Want some company?"

Honey's heart pounded rapidly as she answered. "Sure. Ada is under the weather. I'm giving her some alone time."

"How are you feeling?" Faith asked.

Honey took a deep breath, and wondered, *Why would she ask me how I'm feeling? Could she be suspicious?* "I'm not feeling so hot either, but I'm not as bad off as Ada. Looks like you're doing okay."

"Looks can be deceiving. My stomach is a mess, and I've got a splitting headache. Tina and Rachael have taken residence in their bathrooms, and Amanda is in bed recovering. She gave us a scare earlier, but now seems to be doing better than the rest of us. At first, I thought she must have eaten shrimp, but that would have been impossible since they didn't stop anywhere. Now, I feel she must have had an attack of food poisoning brought on from something we all ate. Who knows? Maybe the breakfast dishes were dirty. Tina is so bad off she's already talking about not walking tomorrow," Faith said.

"If Tina does take the cab, she may have company. Ada's color is closer to green than flesh tone."

Faith sat down. "That soup looks good. I'd order a glass of wine, but I don't think my stomach could take it right now. Rachael may be in that cab, too. Earlier she too was a mild shade of green, but since then her color has turned bright emerald."

"Guess we'll just have to wait until morning to see who will be in good enough shape to walk. Jocelyn left me a message that she plans to be in the lobby by 7:30 a.m." Honey said.

"I'm not sure what's going to happen in the morning. If Tina is still as bad off as she is now, I may have to go with her to our next stop. It took her forever to get down those steps. I don't even want to think about her climbing them in the morning. It's a real shame, too. This is one of the most picturesque towns that we've stayed in. The buildings are so quaint, white buildings, red-tile roofs, and houses built into the sides of the cliff's walls. With the seagulls nestled on the chimney tops, and the sound of the sea in the background, it feels like we've stepped back in time 200 years to an old, magical world," Faith said.

Magical for you, hell for me, thought Honey.

19

SANTANDER TO SANTILLANA DEL MAR (PART ONE)

At 7:30 a.m. Faith went to the hotel lobby. Jocelyn was waiting outside the restaurant entrance.

Jocelyn's initial greeting to Faith was pleasant, "Good morning. How are you, Amanda and Rachael doing this morning? Are you walking today?" Then, her entire mood changed, as she continued with a self-righteous tone in her voice, "I hear Tina isn't feeling well. I'm sure that means she'll be taking the cab. Ada plans to take a cab today as well."

Faith's body stiffened; she held her breath for a count of three. Then, she let her breath out slowly before answering, "Rachael is under the weather. Amanda and I are going to help them get to our next accommodation. From the description, it sounds like we will be staying in another bed-and-breakfast. I'm sure they will need some help getting settled in. Luckily, they seem to be doing better today. Still, I'm going to see if I can find a doctor to see them before we start out today. I talked to a guest at the front desk. Her name is Angela. She's visiting family in town. She told me she knew a doctor and would call and make an appointment for us. I just came down to let you and Honey know that we won't be joining you today. Don't worry about Ada, I'll keep an eye on her, too," Faith said.

Smugly, Jocelyn replied, "Ada won't need your help. Honey and I will see you later."

Faith didn't bother to reply and returned to her room to wait to see whether the guest was able to contact a doctor. When Angela came to her room, Faith couldn't believe her ears.

"I've contacted the doctor. She will arrive within the hour to check on your friends. There won't be a charge for the visit. If you need any medicine, she will give you a prescription and you can purchase what you need at any pharmacy. However, it is customary to tip the doctor to cover their travel expenses," Angela said.

"I can't thank you enough for all your help. This would never happen in the U.S."

Angela wished Faith a good day and left.

When the doctor arrived, Faith couldn't have been more impressed. She was young, considerate, attractive, and knew her business. She diagnosed the girls with food poisoning, administered shots and gave them prescriptions to help reduce the nausea, and regain their electrolyte balance. The doctor said the girls would still be in rough shape, and should take it easy for at least a day. She suggested they skip a day's walk, and remain another day at the hotel. Faith told the doctor that wasn't possible, but that she would accompany them by cab to their next destination.

After the doctor left, it took over an hour for Faith and Amanda to pack and bring the all bags down to the ground floor. Another hour passed before they finished dragging the bags up three blocks of stairs to the only spot level enough for a cab to get to, and were on their way in the cab.

The ordeal from their room to their hotel in Santillana del Mar took most of the morning. With cool rags on Tina's, Rachael's, and Ada's foreheads, they struggled to hold back any chance of vomiting as the cab moved fast, taking sharp turns on the mountain roads.

As the cab rounded a corner, Faith saw what appeared to be a castle in the distance. When the cab pulled up in front, she pulled out her reservation paper and said, "I think you've taken us to the wrong place."

The driver smiled and shook his head, "This is the place."

20

SANTANDER TO SANTILLANA DEL MAR (PART TWO)

After Faith and Amanda had the girls settled into their 9th century parador (castle converted into a hotel) with snacks, water, and medicines by their beds, Faith asked, "Amanda, I saw a *Camino* marker a few miles back on our way here. Did you see it?"

"I did. We could get a cab to take us to that spot."

"I can't think of anything I'd like more," Faith said.

Before calling the cab, they walked out on the veranda, and took in the view of the countryside. Amanda suggested, "Let's get something to eat before we go. The view is too beautiful to waste."

"Good idea."

A hostess greeted them, and although they were dressed in their pilgrim worst, the hostess escorted them as if they were royalty to a fine table.

Faith smiled, "It's going to be tough walking after this."

"Mom, don't be silly. We'll walk faster, and enjoy ourselves all the more. Rachael and I try never to miss afternoon wine when it's available. And it never slows us down."

"That's because you've got youth on your side."

After an enjoyable lunch, the hotel's desk clerk directed a cab driver to take them to an obscure area off the main road where Faith had seen the *Camino* marker.

Faith and Amanda stood in front of the concrete marker and looked into dense foliage. Faith laughed, "Guess this is the place. Remind me, why are we doing this? And after such a lovely lunch, too."

"I'm not sure," Amanda answered.

After pushing their way through some heavy underbrush, they came to a wide meadow filled with bright blue, red, and yellow-colored flowers. The temperature was perfect. Birds sang while monarchs and yellow sulfur butterflies daintily fluttered all around them.

"There must be a thousand butterflies. This is amazing," Amanda said. A smile graced her face when a butterfly landed on her hand.

"This is nice, being together. I'm sorry Tina and Rachael had to miss this beauty, but I have to admit, I've enjoyed our time together."

"Me, too."

"I'm so glad you're okay. I know this is going to sound strange, but somehow I knew that you were in trouble. I saw you were hurt in a vision."

"Sounds a little crazy?" Amanda paused. Faith could see that she was giving careful consideration to her choice of words. Amanda continued, "Mom, we were at such odds with each other after Dad's murder. I blamed you, but I don't anymore. I know it was Dr. Harris who kidnapped me and killed Dad." Amanda took a deep breath, "I never told you, but while I was locked up in that closet, I just knew you and Dad would come to my rescue. What I didn't see, was that Dad would die."

Faith put an arm around Amanda' shoulder, "I'm so sorry you had to go through that."

"Mom, I've never told you how sorry I was that your friend Jackie was murdered. I know how close you two were."

"Thanks hon. That means a lot."

"I can't believe how we trusted Dr. Ivan. A doctor no less."

"We weren't the only ones. There were others."

"Do you think Dad knew he was bad?"

"I'm sure, he didn't. And, I feel your father, at the end, felt as betrayed as did all of Dr. Harris's patients."

"So Mom, how do you think this telepathic stuff works?"

"Think about this. Our brain is like a computer, but a thousand times more complicated. If computers can send messages wirelessly through the air to each other, doesn't it make sense that we could do the same? Did I ever tell you about the day when your great grand-mother died?"

"Maybe, but you know there was a time when I didn't listen to anything you had to say. I may have missed hearing the whole story."

Faith smiled and patted her daughter's shoulder. "You really have grown up, haven't you? So what do you remember?"

"I gather you were close to Grandma. And that you were very young when she died."

"The day she died, I remember we went for a walk. It was a beautiful fall day. We strolled along a path with tall trees. As the sun shown through the leaves they reflected bright oranges, yellows, and reds. The leaves shimmered light gemstones. We came to the creek and sat on the bank. Grandma picked up a handful of clay mud. She handed me some, and we began to make sculptures out of clay. While making our sculptures, she told me a tale about a young girl, Little Feather.

"In the story, Little Feather's parents died from a terrible disease. Sadly she wondered far away from her people. She was ill, too. Lost for many days, she came to a creek, and there she stayed hoping someone would find her. One night before she fell asleep, she made a pony out of mud. The Great Spirit took pity on Little Feather, and in the morning the young girl found her mud pony had come alive. She climbed on the pony's back. It took her to a place where healing herbs grew. Little Feather ate the herbs and her health returned to normal. Her pony took her to the place where her tribe lived. The Chief was so proud of her courage that he adopted her as his own.

"When Grandma finished her story, she took the mud pony I had made from my hands and washed it back into the creek's water. I knew Grandma was telling me something important, but I was too young to understand.

"An eagle appeared overhead. I turned to Grandma, but she was nowhere in sight. And yet, I was not afraid to be there all alone. I watched as the eagle swirled in the air, and danced on the wind. It flew close. I felt as if its eyes were as strong and kind as Grandma's eyes. I felt a strong connection to the eagle. I watched as it flew toward the sun. The light blinded my vision, and when I turned there was Grandma smiling.

"A few years later, I told Mom about my visit with Grandma. She told me that I could not have been with her when she traveled onward with The Great Spirit. Yet, from that moment on whenever I feel sad or alone, I can walk into a quiet place, close my ears, and an eagle appears. It comforts and directs me."

Abruptly Amanda hugged her mother, "I believe you were with her. I never told anyone, but two days after Dad died, I saw him. He appeared in a vision, and told me that he loved me."

Faith held her daughter, "I'm so happy he came to you."

After a few moments of silence, Faith said, "Guess we better get going."

Sometime later, they came to a spot where the castle (their home for the night), could be seen in the distance. As the sun set a radiant mixture of red and orange colors lit up the entire castle. It looked as if it was ablaze.

The sun's rays created brilliant streaks of purple in the sky, and a patchwork of colors graced the countryside. Faith and Amanda strolled along the path, basking in the glory of God's workmanship.

21

SANTILLANA DEL MAR (PART THREE)

The air was cool and dry which provided a great start to a day off. Faith and Amanda sat outside on the terrace enjoying cappuccinos and delicious pancakes. The view in front of them was spectacular. Below the terrace was a rose garden. Beyond they gazed at a countryside dotted by farms creating a checkered collage of colors.

Amanda watched the supple, downy-white clouds glide slowly across the crystal blue sky. "Rachael and Ada are still under the weather. I hope everyone is better by tomorrow. They are missing so much. Rachael would love to sightsee in this town."

Faith nodded understandingly. "If Rachael doesn't recover in time to see the sights, you'll have to take lots of pictures for her. We'll come back to the hotel when we've finished shopping. She might be up to joining us by then," Faith said.

"How's Tina?" Amanda asked.

"She's still very weak. But she said she plans to walk tomorrow."

After breakfast Faith checked on Ada and Tina. Amanda checked on Rachael. All three were sleeping comfortably in their rooms, so Faith and Amanda decided to go to the market.

At the Market they saw Honey and Jocelyn picking over fresh fruits.

When Honey saw Faith and Amanda, she called out, "You've got to try these apples. They're fantastic."

"It's good to see you two are feeling okay," Faith said.

Without looking at Faith, Jocelyn said, "Looks like both of you are feeling better, too."

"Thank goodness. Sure hope the others feel better soon. There is a lot to see in this town. They haven't even felt up to eating out on the veranda at our hotel. The view is spectacular," Faith said.

"It's a nice place, isn't it?" Jocelyn said.

Faith found the sound of Jocelyn's voice pleasant. Happy to see her slightly animated, "You've done a fantastic job finding some really great places to stay. The hotels and bed-and-breakfasts have been wonderful."

"Thanks."

To keep some form of pleasantry between them, Faith looked at Honey and Jocelyn, "Later we plan to see some of the sights. Would you like to join us?"

"Maybe. I'm waiting for a call from home. Until I get the call, I'm going to hang around the hotel," Jocelyn answered.

"I'd love to join you. Come by my room before you go," Honey said. "Who knows, Ada might feel well enough to join us by then."

After Honey and Jocelyn left, Faith and Amanda returned to seeking out tasty fruits and treats. Walking in open-toed sandals, enjoying the freedom from pressure on their blisters, they spent the morning haggling over the prices of delicacies.

Before returning to their rooms, they completed their shopping experience by purchasing large bottles of water, fresh bread, and cheese. "Let's get a bite to eat. Tina, Rachael, and Ada are probably hungry. We can bring back some fresh homemade soup. That should hit the spot," Faith said.

"I can't believe after that wonderful breakfast this morning that I'm ready to eat again, but I'm starving," Amanda said.

After a wonderful lunch and bringing soup back for the others, Faith and Amanda enjoyed a siesta before heading out to tour the town. Rachael and Honey were up to joining them. Jocelyn declined. Tina and Ada were still under-the-weather and did not feel like venturing out.

The first place they chose to visit was the Cloisters of the Collegiate Church.

Inside, Faith admired the main altar. The wall behind the altar rose up to the high ceiling. It was adorned with frescoes edged in gold and silver. Stonework surrounding the altar portrayed legendary battles and images of saints carved in delicate detail. Faith looked out of the corner of her eye at a statue of the Blessed Virgin and smiled, remembering when she challenged God to prove His existence. She couldn't believe she still had hopes that a statue would wink at her.

The four, lost in their personal thoughts, moved slowly around the cathedral. They separated, each drawn to artifacts targeting their individual interests.

Outside, they regrouped and stepped into a corridor which opened into a large courtyard. Columns along the corridor were ornamented at the top with similar Corinthian carvings and Acanthus leaf designs like those seen inside the church. Rachael looked into the courtyard, "Isn't this garden area beautiful? The flowers and bushes are so colorful."

Individually, each member of the group agreed with Rachael's comment.

Faith lingered a moment, then released a long breath, "Tina would have loved this place."

"I'm sure this won't be the last chapel we're going to encounter on this trip, especially since the path takes us from one church to the next," Honey said.

"We've seen the outside of a lot of churches, but so many have been closed when we passed by. It seems many close their doors between services. With closed churches, overgrown paths, and not seeing very many other pilgrims, there are times I wonder if we will ever meet other pilgrims on this trip," Rachael said.

"I'm sure as we get closer to the French route we will see more pilgrims. Ready to visit the caves?" Faith asked.

In unison, Amanda and Rachael answered. "Ready."

The entrance to the cave was on top of a hill. When they reached the top 30 minutes later, Faith pointed down the hill. "At least the walk home will be pleasant."

Amanda laughed, "You know we've been gone too long when you start calling a hotel home."

Inside the cave, Rachael picked up a brochure and read, "In 1879, amateur archaeologist Marcelino Sanz de Sautuola, with his nine-year-old daughter by his side, discovered the cave's drawings. Because of the exceptional state of conservation of the paintings, Sautuola was accused of forgery. Years later, the Altamira Caves were authenticated, but by then Sautuola, had already died, and did not live to enjoy his reputation's vindication.

"During the 1960s and 1970s, the paintings became damaged by carbon dioxide from the breath of so many admiring visitors. Altamira was closed to the public in 1977, but reopened with limited access in 1982. The caves were replicated in exact detail for tourists to walk through in order to save the originals." Rachael pointed. "You can see the original caves through this glass wall. This place is absolutely amazing. You can picture women cooking, children playing, and families sitting around campfires. It feels really comfortable inside this cave. It's huge."

After their visit on the way down the hill, conversation was filled with laughter as they reflected on some of their close-call events.

"I was using our usual bathroom facility, the corn field, when I heard the owner of the farm checking his crop. He was only two or three rows from me. I almost passed-out holding my breath so as not to be discovered," Rachael said.

"That's not as bad as the day I stepped out of the shower only to discover two men playing cards outside my window staring at me. It wouldn't have been so bad, if they had looked at least a little surprised. Instead they just waved, and wished me a good evening," Amanda said.

When the group returned to the hotel, and Honey entered her room, she was in a complete state of flux. She had enjoyed Faith and Amanda's company. Now, listening to Ada moan and groan, desperation set in. Honey cringed. She needed to clear her head and figure out a new plan for getting rid of Amanda. Since her first plan didn't work, she would move to Plan B.

"Ada, I'm going to step outside for a breath of fresh air. Do you need anything?"

"Not right now. Thanks."

While looking for a place to get a drink, Honey remembered that they would be traveling through gypsy country again? If she killed Amanda near one of their camps, suspicions would fall on the gypsies.

That evening Ada joined Jocelyn and Honey for dinner at the hotel's restaurant. Ada was still feeling rough and sipped her soup slowly.

"Ada, do you think you'll be up to walking tomorrow?" Jocelyn asked.

"I'm feeling much better. I still feel a little queasy, but I'm feeling good enough to walk."

With Ada in a weakened state, Honey felt it was the perfect time to ask, "Do you think we will be going through gypsy country again?"

With a look of concern, Ada asked the waiter. "Is there any chance that we will be encountering gypsies?"

The waiter smiled as if it were a ridiculous question. "They camp and move all around these hills, but they're harmless. They don't like to bring attention to themselves."

Ada shook her head when the waiter left the table. "That's what he thinks."

Hearing this, Honey thought, *Perfect.*

Following dinner, with thoughts still focused on her plan, Honey found an outdoor café. She sat at a table, and ordered a glass of wine. She noticed a young couple sitting at a table close by. The young man's sweetheart pulled a cigarette out of her purse. As she brought the cigarette to her lips, the young man quickly used his lighter to light her cigarette. Sitting in an outdoor café, the gesture seemed very romantic. The glow of the lighter's flame reflected a warm glow in the young woman's glass of red wine. Honey's thoughts drifted to Ivan. She wished he was there.

Lost in thought, Honey missed Rachael's approach.

"Decompressing?" Rachael asked. Honey's body jerked. "Sorry. I didn't mean to surprise you."

With a weak smile, Honey said, "No problem. Are you girls going out on the town this evening?"

"I don't think we will. Everyone is still a little under the weather. Amanda is with her Mom. Tina talked about skipping tomorrow and if I'm not better, I may join her. My stomach is still causing me some trouble. I want to get over this thing for good. I came down to get some juice."

Reluctantly, Honey offered, "Want to join me?"

"Sure."

Hoping to avoid revealing her true feelings, Honey graciously accepted Rachael's intrusion, and used the occasion for reconnaissance. To create a little added anxiety over the following day's hike, she said, "I hear we might be traveling through gypsy country again tomorrow. Better tell Amanda and Faith to keep their eyes open."

"I will."

Honey took a chance an asked, "Ada and Jocelyn have mentioned more than once that Amanda's father was killed under violent circumstances a couple of years ago. Do you think running into gypsies might bring up old bad memories?"

Honey could see the surprised look on Rachael's face. Her response was short and there was a definite sarcastic tone as she answered, "I guess those gals must have run out of things to talk about. It wasn't just her father. Amanda was kidnapped, and Faith's best friend was murdered, too. Amanda couldn't even talk to me about it for a long time. It's only recently that she's felt comfortable. The whole ordeal took its toll on both Faith and Amanda. It even caused a bit of a riff in their relationship, but they're doing better now. Still, Amanda doesn't like to talk about the event around people she doesn't know. She might find running into gypsies worrisome, but I really think she's past all that. Besides, I think most gypsies are okay. I think our previous encounter was out of the ordinary."

Now curious after hearing Faith had a friend who was murdered around the same time, Honey commented, "I don't remember reading anything about a murder. I mean, usually the press is all over a story like that."

"The police tried to keep it quiet. They suspected the killer was responsible for other deaths, and they didn't want their investigation messed up," Rachael said.

Heat rose to Honey's face, *Lies. Lies. Nothing but lies.*

Santilla del Mar

22

SANTILLANA DEL MAR TO COMILLAS

Up early to get a jump on the day, Honey heard a cab's engine sputtering as it came down the road. She knew it was for them. It was too early in the morning for any respectable Spaniard to be awake.

When the cab parked outside Honey's window, she could hear the conversation between the cab driver and the hotel's concierge. Listening to the receptionist explain the number of passengers and the bag situation kept Honey entertained while she contemplated more serious matters. After she saw who would be walking, she'd be able to determine if today would be a good day to complete her task.

Faith and Tina brought down their luggage. Based on Tina's casual attire, Honey concluded she did not plan to walk.

Ada announced, "I've been up all night with the runs. I'm going with Tina."

Jocelyn looked at Honey. "I'm leaving right after breakfast."

Hesitantly Honey answered, "I'll be ready."

Jocelyn looked at Faith. "What about you?"

"I'm going to wait for Amanda. I'm sure we'll see each other during the day."

Amanda and Rachael came down to breakfast as the rest were finishing. Honey quickly decided that the day looked like it could turn out to be a good day after all.

The exodus began. Each put her bag into the cab. Tina and Ada got in as Honey and Jocelyn started off down the street. Honey looked back. Good! As usual Rachael and Amanda were taking their time. Her plan wouldn't work if they caught up to her too soon.

Within the first hour, the path took Honey and Jocelyn over uneven treacherous ground covered with almost impenetrable forest. Honey looked back to see if the others were in sight. It was hard to see through the trees and bushes, but at this point they were still out of sight.

Honey and Jocelyn made their way out of the forest where the aroma of eucalyptus had pervaded. Cows raised their heads as if to say their lazy day was being interrupted by this intrusion.

Leaving the meadow, Honey looked back. It didn't appear they were racing to catch up to them. From this point, the ground they walked was wet from the previous night's rain, and they slipped over cobblestones into the next hamlet.

Jocelyn noticed a bar. "It looks like that place is open. I could sure stand getting something cool to drink."

Honey did not want to slow down. She hoped the bar would be closed.

To Honey's dismay, the bar was open. While sipping her soft drink, she looked out the open door. Disappointed, she saw the others making their way through town. Before Jocelyn and Honey were ready to start out again, Faith and the girls entered the bar.

"Isn't this town adorable?" Amanda asked.

Jocelyn arched her eyebrows. "You can tell who's young and energetic, can't you? You should try their sandwiches. The one that looks like salami with melted cheese is the one I had."

"Sounds good," Amanda replied.

Faith, Amanda, and Rachael joined Honey and Jocelyn. They drank soft drinks and chatted while waiting for their sandwiches to be heated.

When Jocelyn and Honey finished, they stood up and put on their backpacks, and Jocelyn announced, "I'm sure you gals will catch up with us again somewhere along the way."

"If we don't, we'll see you later this evening. We're taking it easy today," Faith said.

At the outskirts of town, Honey and Jocelyn found the *Camino* marker. From there they made their way through farmlands filled with corn stalks, ready for harvest, and traveled trails so overgrown that the trail markers were almost undiscoverable. At the crossroads, after shoving bushes aside, Honey found the arrow marker carved into a stone. As Jocelyn started up the path, Honey decided that this crossroads would fit into her plan. She hadn't seen any sign of the others for some time now.

"Jocelyn, something's in my shoe. I need to stop a minute." Honey knew Jocelyn wouldn't wait.

"I'll see you in a bit," Jocelyn said.

As soon as Jocelyn was out of sight, Honey pushed the stone marker into a gully, out of view. She found a rock to sit on, and waited.

When Faith saw Honey, she called out, "Are you okay? Did something happen?"

"No. No. I'm fine. I stopped to get something out of my shoe at the last bend, and Jocelyn continued onward. I must have taken a wrong turn. I haven't seen her since. Now, I'm all turned around and can't decide which way to go. Maybe if we each go out a short distance, in different directions, one of us will find the marker," Honey said.

Amanda and Rachael wasted no time heading out in different directions. Faith waited, and asked, "Which path were you on?"

With a look of concern on her face, Honey pointed, "I think I went that way, but I can't be certain. Maybe I should wait here. At least that will give us a starting point."

When Faith and Rachael were out of sight, Honey followed Amanda. As soon as Amanda was in sight, she pulled the filled poison syringe from her pack, and held it close to her body, out of sight.

Amanda turned, and asked. "Honey, how did you wind up on this path?"

Honey smiled and moved in closer. "The trails must all merge at some point."

Now within range to take action, Honey put her thumb on the syringe. She was raising her arm when a voice from behind stopped her.

"How'd we all wind up at this point?" Rachael asked.

Honey quickly lowered her arm, and slowly tucked the syringe into her backpack, while thinking, *Squelched again.*

Together the three walked back to the crossroads. Faith stood there waiting. "What happened to you girls? Honey, I thought you were going to wait here?"

"I had an idea that the paths might circle back on each other. I decided to check out my theory." Honey answered.

"That leaves only one path left for us to take. Onward we go," Faith said.

23

COMILLAS TO LLANES

The next day all seven were feeling good and ready to travel. Honey successfully hid her frustrations under the cover of pleasant conversation. As the day progressed, conversation decreased as fatigue set in. This gave Honey plenty of quiet time to toss ideas around in her mind as to how to deal with Amanda.

She heard Amanda and Rachael coming up the path behind her around lunchtime. They were talking and giggling the whole way. It was clear to Honey that their day's experience was much different from hers. She felt tense. Anger permeated every part of her body.

When Rachael saw Jocelyn, she said, "I guess you saw the marker pointing straight up the electric pole. It was nowhere near a path and I didn't think we were supposed to climb that pole. If it wasn't for a man taking his bull for a walk, we never would have figured out the way. How did you gals figure it out?"

Not wanting to give the girls the satisfaction of discovering that they had gone the wrong way, Jocelyn answered smugly, "Just lucky, I guess."

Amanda and Rachael walked with Honey and the others for about 30 minutes. "We're going to take a break. Catch up with you later," Rachael said.

For a moment, Honey thought about making an excuse to stay with them, but then reconsidered. They were moving into more populated areas. In a few days they'd return to mountainous areas. She felt her chances would be better then.

An hour later, Honey's group entered a place where condominiums and a freeway were under construction. The three searched for a *Camino* marker, but found none.

"I can't believe this. We're going to have to walk this entire ledge to find a marker," Jocelyn said harshly.

"Look. I'll climb up to the top of this embankment," Honey volunteered. When she reached the top, from that vantage point, she saw a yellow arrow down in the ravine on the other side of railroad tracks. She took a deep breath, observing the tracks were bordered by concrete walls.

When she rejoined Jocelyn and Ada, she explained the situation. "We will have to climb over a concrete wall, cross the tracks, then climb up and out over the second concrete wall to the other side."

"How can this be?" Jocelyn said.

"The paths on this section of the *Camino* obviously have not been traveled much. The paths continue to cross areas where new development is surfacing. I'm sure workers in these areas aren't aware that they are often destroying *Camino* trails. Let's just get to the other side. When we get to the next spot where our *Camino* passports are stamped, we can tell someone of our challenges." Honey suddenly realized the tone of her voice denoted agitation and had increased several octaves. Her next words were spoken with control. "Okay, we're all tired and getting across these tracks is going to be difficult. Let's just take a minute to figure this out."

Ada took off her backpack, picked up three small tree branches and laid them out to form an arrow.

In a restless tone, Jocelyn said, "Ada, what are you doing?"

"Letting the others know which way to go. I'm almost done."

When they reached the first wall, Ada, Honey and Jocelyn lowered their backpacks over it before letting them drop to the ground.

Honey was the first to climb down the concrete wall. She had to release her hands from the wall and drop the last few feet to the ground. The drop was farther than Honey had anticipated. Hitting the ground, she felt a twinge of pain as her right ankle buckled. *Great, this is all I need.*

Jocelyn saw Honey limping across the tracks to the next wall. "Are you okay?"

"I'll let you know after we get up and out of here. We'd be in big trouble if a train comes along right about now."

"You got that right," Ada said.

Honey found a spot where small crevices in the wall provided enough leverage for her to climb up the second wall. When she was secure on the ledge she leaned over so Ada and Jocelyn could hand up their packs to her. Ada and Jocelyn climbed out and they were soon continuing on the trail.

"Honey, are you okay?" Ada asked.

"I think I sprained my ankle, but I'll be okay."

"I hope it's not bad," Ada said.

Amanda and Rachael soon came to the arrow Ada had left for them. "It was sure nice of them to leave this marker, but getting across these tracks isn't going to be easy." Rachael said.

"That's for sure."

After the girls had their backpacks off, but before tossing them over the wall, Amanda asked, "How will Tina ever make it over this wall?"

"Not easily, that's for sure," Rachael said.

"Maybe we should wait until they catch up to us. We might be able to help Tina across."

More than an hour passed before Tina and Faith caught up to Amanda and Rachael. When Faith saw the girls sitting on the concrete wall, she anxiously called out, "Did something happen?"

"No Mom, we're fine, but there is a problem with the trail."

Rachael pointed down to the railroad track. "This is where we are supposed to cross."

Tina moved to the edge of the concrete wall. "Oh, my God. I can't do this."

Faith stood beside Tina. "Yes, you can."

Tina and Faith removed their backpacks. Faith watched Tina try to get footing on the wall. Suddenly, she stopped. "I'm not doing this. If I fall, I'll never be able to get out of there. I'm going back to the last town and get a ride. It's not worth me trying this."

Faith's breathing strained as she tried repeatedly to convince Tina to continue.

Rachael intervened. "Tina's right. We're really close, and this crossing is dangerous."

Visibly upset, Faith agreed. Forcefully, she put on her backpack, and waited for Tina to do the same. "You two, be careful," Faith shouted to the girls. "We'll wait here until you are safely across before heading back."

Amanda and Rachael tossed their backpacks over the wall, then climbed down the wall, and made their way across the railroad tracks. After they were up and over the second concrete wall, Faith and Tina retreated to find transportation. Back on the trail, at a construction site Faith asked a young man where they could find a cab. He told them finding a cab would be impossible, but after they told him they were going to Llanes, he told them where they could catch a bus that would take them there.

They followed his instructions and a short time later they came to a rundown glass-enclosed cubicle with a bench inside. "This must be the place," Faith said.

While they waited, Faith noted it was a gorgeous day. The distance to the hotel was short, and she knew the way. After Tina was on the bus, she'd return to the path and finish the day's walk.

In the distance, Faith watched dirt swirl around a large moving vehicle. "Here comes your ride."

Surprised, Tina asked, "What do you mean, 'My ride'? Aren't you coming with me?"

"Not this time. We're close and I know the way," Faith answered.

Tina's voice cracked. "But crossing those tracks is going to be dangerous."

"Nonsense. I saw how they got across. Stop worrying. I'll be fine."

Tina boarded the bus. Faith waved a pleasant good-bye and resumed her walk. When she reached the all-too-familiar concrete wall, and began the challenge of crossing, she felt disconcerted as her arms trembled as she held on going down. Her hands were still shaking so much when she got to the other side it took her three tries to toss her backpack up onto the second ledge.

When she made it over that wall, her nerves calmed. She slung on her backpack and reclaimed the pleasure of listening to cowbells ringing in the fields, and the sight of horses trotting up to fences to greet her along the way. Blissful in the serenity of the hush of the forest, Faith came to a crossroads at the top of a ridge. Searching for a yellow arrow and finding none, she looked down into the valley, and saw a large building with a blue roof. She decided that since it was the only large building in sight, it must be their hotel.

One path looked as if it followed level ground; the other looked as if it went down into the village. Faith started to take the downward path when she was stopped by the loud, strange sound of a donkey bellowing, "Hee Haw, Hee Haw!"

The donkey appeared to be alone on the trail. It also seemed to be warning her not to take the path in the direction she was going, but instead invited her to follow.

Faith took an apple out of her pack, and cautiously approached the animal. As she did, the donkey quieted. She turned her hand upward with her fingers curved back and offered the donkey the apple. While it ate, Faith looked into its eyes. "So, Mr. Donkey are you traveling the *Camino* or are you simply out for a stroll?"

As expected, the donkey did not answer, and continued down the path. Together they strolled. When the donkey made a right-hand turn at the crossroads, Faith patted the donkey's neck. "It's been a pleasure walking with you, but I think the other path will take me to my hotel."

As soon as she turned to leave, as if the donkey understood what she'd said, it brayed loudly. Then, its head nudged the back of her shoulder, as if to say, "No, come this way."

Faith looked at the donkey. "I must be crazy," she said aloud. She walked with her new companion for an hour. She became fearful she was going the wrong way. "I'm not sure you're heading where I need to go. It's not that you haven't been great company; it's just your home may not take me close to where I need to go." Then a thought struck her. If she went with the donkey to its home, the owner could direct her to the right path.

Suddenly, the donkey turned and made a quick right into a fenced yard.

Faith looked around and discovered she was standing on a plateau, then, looked at her friend, the donkey. "Guess you're home?" Behind the donkey, she saw the top floor of a building built into the side of the cliff where she now stood. She assumed the building had been constructed tall enough to reach the plateau. While observing this unique construction, a door opened. A woman dressed in a uniform of a housecleaner stepped out into the field. The woman smiled at Faith, and in Spanish asked, "Are you staying with us?"

Surprised by the question, Faith walked to the edge of the cliff and looked down. The building was a hotel, and through the restaurant's glass window, she could see Tina, Rachael, and Amanda sitting at a table. Seeing Faith, Tina instantly stood, went to the window, and signaled for her to come down. Faith shrugged her shoulders indicating that the climb down was too steep. The woman, now standing with the donkey, signaled for Faith to follow her.

By way of the hammered tin door on the back side of the top floor of the hotel, Faith worked her way down seven flights of stairs. Eventually she found her way to the lobby where she found her daughter and friends waiting.

"How did you ever find this place?" Tina asked. "None of the others could find it. Amanda and Rachael almost gave up. Then, one of the town's folk saw they were lost and walked them to the hotel. Jocelyn and her crew arrived in a cab. After they reached the town, and after walking in ten different directions and still not finding anyone who could tell them where this place was located, they found a driver who knew where to go. When Jocelyn got out of the cab, she looked more frustrated than at any other time I've seen her on this trip. My bus took me to the front door," Tina said smugly.

Faith smiled coyly. "I followed a donkey. We developed a sort-of understanding."

Tina laughed, "Somehow, I'm not surprised."

"I'm sure glad you found that donkey, Mom."

"Me, too," Faith said.

Exhausted, all seven called it an early evening. The following morning when Faith looked out her window she saw speckles of light touching the leaves on trees. A cool breeze caressed her cheek, and she heard her friend the donkey braying. To Faith it sounded like, *"Bon Camino."*

After breakfast, the entire group crossed the street, entered the forest, and proceeded to zigzag their way through growth that was taller than two men. The difference between yesterday and this day was the ground was so wet, and the vegetation so tall, that the group had to travel at relatively the same pace. It wasn't until they moved into a more populated area where summer homes, condos, and vacation apartments were staggered along the shoreline, that Jocelyn's group once again picked up speed and separated from the others.

Amanda and Rachael continued at a slower pace, keeping company with Tina and Faith. Late afternoon they came to an opening where they saw a small village a short distance down the road. "We could hit that town in time to have lunch before things shut down," Rachael suggested.

"That would be great. With some food in my belly, I'm sure I can finish the day with the rest of you," Tina replied.

In town, they happily found a restaurant open. Before they entered the restaurant, shoelaces were loosened to let tired feet relax while they ate. They were greeted warmly and seated quickly. The four enjoyed their meals and shared laughter about incidents experienced on the trip, which at the time seemed horrible, but now were treasures of amusement. For the first time on their adventure, Faith noticed that Tina looked at ease.

After lunch, they traveled along the sides of moss-covered stonewalls. Trees arched over the pathways. One tree was so large, within its hollow base it encompassed a small table and chairs.

"I feel as if we are walking through a fairytale land. I could picture Alice from *Alice in Wonderland* sitting at the table in the tree trunk," Amanda said.

As they continued their trek, it began to rain. Soon soaking wet and covered in mud, Faith thought, *Tina's doing really well, and I'm with my daughter. Even with the rain, this has turned out to be a great day.*

24

LLANES TO OVIEDO

Torturous, sleepless nights on the *Camino* had occurred more times than Faith wanted to remember. Interruptions ranged from sounds of merriment outside her bedroom window to poor ventilation inside their room.

Last night's stay had been a glorious exception. Their bed-and-breakfast, located in the countryside, away from civilization was nothing short of heavenly. She lay in bed listening to birds singing and a rooster crowing. The aroma of fresh-brewed coffee, bacon and eggs drifted into her room. Faith had been given the single bed in the loft to sleep in. It was placed by an open window with a perfect view of last evening's full moon and the surrounding countryside. This was the first time on the trip Faith had a room to herself. The bed was firm and her pillow soft. Cool air entered her room. She savored the coolness against her face, as she took a deep breath, smiled, then sat up. She looked out the loft window. The sun seemed to shine brighter and the air even smelled fresher than previous days. She thanked God. On mornings like this, the purpose of suffering was clear to her. She wouldn't appreciate the touch of the wind, or the joys of nature's heavenly perfume, without having lost them through the pain of fatigue.

When Faith went downstairs, she found the table was set with fine china. Crystal glasses were filled with fresh-squeezed orange juice.

Faith saw the owner step into the adjoining room. The woman placed clothes she'd washed, dried, and folded for them the night before on a table in the corner of the room. Once again she would begin her day wearing clothes not washed in a tub or sink. She thanked the owner of the bed and breakfast for doing their wash. Faith knew she must have stayed up half the night doing their laundry.

The seven sat for breakfast. "Last night I had the best night's sleep I've ever had," Rachael said.

"Me too," Jocelyn said.

"Clean clothes, sunshine, and cool temperatures. What a glorious way to start the day!" Ada said.

After breakfast their host handed them bread, cheese, fruit, water and sandwiches to take with them on their day's journey.

Tina hugged the lovely woman of the house, *"Muchas Gracias."*

"We can't thank you enough," Faith said.

Less excitedly, Honey added, "Thanks. It should be a good day."

"Thanks to your wonderful hospitality, I feel great. Plus, my feet don't hurt, and I weighed myself on your scale this morning. I've lost 25 pounds. I am ready for anything," Tina said enthusiastically.

Faith's body tensed. She waited for words of sarcasm. None came.

"That's great," Amanda said.

"Good job," Ada added.

With clean clothes packed and full bellies, no one complained about the late start to the day. A sense of well-being persisted as they hiked over rolling hills and open meadows. By lunchtime, the natural order of things had them separated into three groups.

Honey, Jocelyn, and Ada found a wonderful family-owned restaurant at an overlook. The day was so pleasant they hung out at the restaurant and waited for Amanda and Rachael to catch up and join them for lunch.

After Amanda and Rachael arrived, and before the group had finished ordering their meal, to everyone's surprise, Faith and Tina strolled into the restaurant.

During lunch Jocelyn looked across the table at Faith, "I can't believe you haven't gotten lost on this trip."

Honey looked at Jocelyn surprise by her comment.

Faith smiled. "Honey, you haven't been around when I've gotten lost. I've taken a few unnecessary detours on other trips. The rest of the group has experienced first hand my propensity for getting lost. If you put me in my own backyard and turn me around, I'll get lost. I've been that way my whole life, but I've reached a point that I am actually comfortable in this state. Since I gave up worrying where I'm heading, I find I am much more capable of living in the moment. I actually find my way faster when I'm not anxious about getting lost."

Faith tapped her finger against her cheek and with a thoughtful look said, "Jocelyn, I've only gotten lost once on this trip. These yellow arrows are a blessing. I seem to have no problem finding the *Camino* markers. I may not know where I am, but I can tell which way to go."

"Amanda, do you remember the day your mom was taking us to that Macy's grand opening? She got so lost we wound up two towns away. It got to be so late that she had to get a hotel room for the night. The following day, she made the best of it by taking us shopping. After that, every time your mom said she was going shopping, all our girlfriends wanted to go," Rachael said.

"Better stop your teasing. You could jinx her near perfect record," Tina said.

Following a magnificent lunch, the *Camino* reclaimed its mastery over the group. Feet burned, backs ached, and, before long, Tina and Faith were once again separated from the rest. But this day, despite the fact that Tina's breathing remained strained on the uphill climbs, her spirits never waned.

They turned a corner and found a small plot of land filled with vegetable gardens. Nearby, they saw small cottages with front porches and flower beds. A small chapel was within walking distance to the cottages. Surprisingly, next to the chapel was a bar with the word INN written above the door.

"Do you think we are staying in those cottages?" Tina asked.

Faith looked at her list of names where they were scheduled to stay. She laughed. "I do believe this is it. We are staying at 'The Inn'. I thought it was a joke when I read it."

Upon entering the bar, they were greeted by Amanda and Rachael.

"You gals look refreshed. Guess you've been here awhile," Tina said.

"Not that long. We just finished showering. You'll like this place. The rooms are great, but the restaurant isn't really set up for regular meals. They serve food only after Mass. Lucky for us there is a service this evening. The owner said they will be serving a chicken dish. The others are resting in their rooms until dinner. The bar has some snacks we can pack for breakfast and lunch. The owner told us that there isn't much between here and where we are going tomorrow," Rachael said.

"Have you girls checked out the chapel?" Faith asked.

"We did. You won't believe the tile works inside, and the stained glass windows. We just peeked in. There were a few people inside praying. We didn't want to go in until we were cleaned up," Amanda said.

After a long shower and dressing for dinner, Faith opened the door and started to step outside, then paused. "Tina, are you dressed?"

"Yes. Is something wrong?"

"No, come quickly. Look!"

Faith pointed to the road. They saw men on horseback, donkey carts loaded with people, and lone individuals traveling the road, making their way to the chapel all dressed in their Sunday best.

"This is unbelievable. I would have never thought there were so many people living in these hills," Tina said.

All of a sudden, every horse, cart, and pedestrian moved to the side of the road to let a car pass. When the car stopped, a priest stepped out. The procession continued. Horses were hitched to railings and carts were parked. Walkers greeted the priest with smiles and handshakes. A procession formed behind him, and they all entered the chapel.

Faith saw Jocelyn and signaled, "Let's go." Jocelyn nodded.

Inside the chapel, Faith and Tina sat in the back. Amanda sat next to her mother. Faith's hand lightly patted Amanda's knee. Amanda put her hand on Faith's. Faith smiled, *Thank you, God.*

The evening could not have been more glorious. After the service, the seven joined the entire community for the Spanish version of chicken and dumplings. They laughed, drank wine, and later, each used their calling cards to phone home from the bar.

Faith's call home to Tom was short, especially since she couldn't get too mushy with the entire town sitting in the bar listening in, and with Amanda sitting by her side. "Hi, Tom. How are you?" Faith said.

"I'm great, except for missing you. You sounded down the last time we spoke. I wanted to come over there and bring you home."

"Oh, I'm doing much better."

"You sound better."

"We're nearing the French route. I'm expecting things will continue to improve."

"Glad to hear it. I miss you. How's Amanda? And where are you? Sounds like a party going on in the background," Tom asked.

"As a matter of fact, we are in a bar. Jealous?"

Tom laughed, "Of you in a bar? Maybe, but not of your trip."

Faith lowered her voice, "I miss you, too." Then in a louder tone, she added. "Amanda is doing great."

Amanda leaned into the phone, "Hi, Tom. When friends call, tell them we're having a wonderful time."

"Talk to you soon. I miss you," Faith said as she hung up the phone.

Faith looked at Amanda. "So, you're having a wonderful time, too?"

Amanda smiled, "Well, most of the time, but my friends don't need to know all is not rosy."

Over the next few days, the group traveled through Ribadesella, Colunga, and Villaviciosa with one thought in mind, getting to Oviedo for a day of rest.

For weeks, Faith awoke each morning wondering if Tina was going to walk, since every night before sleeping, Tina would say, "I'm not doing this again. I'm going with the cab." Then, in the morning she would change her mind, and walk. Now, with Tina completing each day, and having conquered overgrown forests and mountains, Faith felt confident in Tina's resolve to finish the pilgrimage.

On the outskirts of Oviedo, they came to a point where they could see the town in the distance. The path took them along side a stream. Cheerfully, Faith said, "Beautiful, isn't it?"

Tina nodded, but Faith saw the concerned look on her face. Oviedo was still hours away. Tina remained quiet over the next two hours. Faith saw fatigue written all over Tina's face. But after they found a restaurant open, and stopping to eat and rest, Faith watched her energy return. Now in the region of Auturia they dined on cheese served with fresh greens, covered with hazelnuts swimming in a light vinaigrette and virgin olive oil. With the addition of complimentary wine and freshly baked bread, they made it to town with smiles on their faces.

25

OVIEDO

Faith and Tina took advantage of their rest day in Oviedo, and slept in until the town residents awoke.

"Next time I do this, I'm traveling on Spanish time. If I'm going to be kept awake by listening to everyone having fun at night, I'm going to join them, sleep in and start late," Faith said.

"Take a few extra days so we could travel shorter distances each day," Tina added.

"That sounds good, too. There's a lot to see in this town. Where do you want to go first?" Faith asked.

"Breakfast! You've got too much energy. I'll check out some of the sights, but I plan to rest a good chunk of the day," Tina said.

Faith smiled, "Touchy, touchy. No problem."

At a nearby café, Faith and Tina consumed cappuccinos, and egg-and-bacon tapas. From where they sat they could see a life-sized statue of a mother with her child. They left the restaurant and walked to the statue. Tina handed Faith her camera, and took her place beside the statue. "Can you take my picture? I'll take yours next."

Tina pointed. "Look, there's another statue of two kids playing. Every which way you look, another statue can be seen. Let's check them out."

"Thought you were going to rest?" Faith remarked.

"I will, later. I just know you and how you won't stop until you drop," Tina said.

"Hey, there's Honey. We should ask her to join us," Faith said.

"Here we go," Tina said.

After hooking up with Honey, and checking out several of the town's sculptures, Tina said her good-byes. "I'm heading back to the room. See you later."

"See you later," Faith repeated.

"So, where are Amanda and Rachael?" Honey asked.

"They went out last night. But even after staying up late, they were up and out before Tina and me this morning."

"Jocelyn and Ada left word that they had found a place which offers massages. They've scheduled massages in their rooms at the hotel. I might schedule one later," Honey said.

"Want to check out Oviedo's Cathedral?" Faith asked.

"Sure."

Entering The Cathedral of Oviedo, Faith noticed carvings covered in gold-leaf and colorful frescos. She walked to the center aisle, and facing the altar, said, "My friend Jackie would have loved this trip."

"Bad timing for her to join you?" Honey asked.

Faith's body went limp. She found a bench and sat down. "She's dead. Murdered."

"Want to talk about it?" Honey asked.

The cheerless look on Faith's face accompanied her answer, "Maybe later."

As they sat in silence, Honey felt sincerity in Faith's report of the loss of her friend. Her attentions went to thoughts of her best friend, her elder sister of three years. Margie had also died at the hands of violence. Honey thought about how much her sister would have loved this trip, too.

Margie had been Honey's protector. When their father drank, he would always beat them, but Margie was always there to block the blow when he came for Honey. She looked at the cross on the altar thinking if only Margie hadn't hidden her that night, he wouldn't have gotten so mad. And she'd still be with her.

Honey turned. Faith's eyes were closed. Her hands folded in prayer. Honey shook her head in disgust thinking, if Faith hadn't framed Ivan for her ex-husband's murder, she wouldn't have to kill Amanda.

When Honey looked back to the altar, a bright light streamed through the stained-glass window above the altar. She felt a presence. She closed her eyes wishing she had been with her sister the night she died. She remembered the last words Margie spoke as she closed the door to the shelter. "Dad's wrong. We're good girls."

Their father went to prison, and Honey bounced from foster home to foster home. She never spoke of her past until she began therapy with Dr. Ivan Harris.

Honey's stomach churned as she remembered her sister's words, *We're good girls.*

Suddenly feeling exhausted, Honey said. "Faith, I'm going to head back to schedule a massage. Want me to see if I can schedule one for you?"

Faith opened her eyes. "No thanks, but I'll walk back with you. I'd like to see if Amanda is around. Hope you're not skipping out because of my poor company?"

"Not at all, it's simply, I'm all about getting my feet rubbed."

"I'm not sure anyone would touch my feet as bad as they are right now. They've never looked this bad," Faith said.

When Faith and Honey neared the hotel, they passed a café. Amanda ran out, "Mom, we've been looking for you. Tina's getting her hair done. We made an appointment for you. How do you like our new hairdos?" Amanda asked.

Honey waved and said, "Good luck."

Faith stared at the pink-and-purple streaks in Amanda's and Rachael's new hair styles. Hesitantly, Faith answered, "It's different."

That evening at mealtime, conversation revolved around the day's adventures of each person while waiters held pitchers of apple cider to the height of their heads and poured the cider freely into glasses on the table. Most of the time, the cider filled the glasses, but occasionally their aim was off. Soon, cider glistened on the floor of the restaurant. At times, it spilled onto patrons, too.

While the group enjoyed watching the waiters entertain their patrons, cider splashed onto Ada's back. Ada jerked.

"Are you okay?" Rachael asked.

"I'm fine. Getting splashed with cider isn't nearly as embarrassing as was my massage earlier today. The masseuse was young, very cute, and male. Being alone in the room with him, I could hardly breathe under the spell of his heavenly hands. That was until my snoring woke me," Ada answered.

"Hey, there are young girls listening," Jocelyn said. "Besides, my masseuse was large and blond. She looked like she was from Sweden."

Jocelyn and Ada pulled out shopping bags and showed their treasures of new socks and underwear, while Amanda, Rachael, Tina, and Faith showed off their new hairdos and colorful locks of hair.

After dinner, they pulled out topographic maps to review the trail.

Jocelyn looked directly at Tina before she spoke. "It looks like we will be walking along narrow rock ledges along the cliff's face, and climbing all day."

"Thanks for the warning," Faith said.

"Can I take a look?" Honey asked.

Viewing the map, and seeing the prediction of a challenging day had not been exaggerated, Honey's confidence in achieving her goal increased.

26

OVIEDO TO AVILES

At dawn, Honey climbed out of bed and walked to the open window. Dampness filled the air, and the land leading to Aviles was covered in a thick, heavy fog. It was so thick she couldn't even see the cottage next to hers.

Ada sat up in bed. "Looks like rain. Guess we will need to put the rubber tips on our poles when we hit pavement."

"I don't expect this paved road to go on very far before we are back out into woods. I haven't put rubber tips on my poles for days. I can't even remember where I put them," Honey said.

"Don't worry. I've got extras. The owner said she'd meet us at the bar this morning. She didn't seem happy about getting up to serve us, but agreed. She said he'd have some fruit and cereal for us to eat for breakfast. This place, like most, doesn't open for breakfast," Ada said.

At the bar the group was greeted with a big smile from the proprietor. She was plump, and wore a cotton print dress with an embroidered apron. She apologized for having nothing more than orange juice, coffee, and cereal for breakfast.

The fact that there were fresh cappuccinos and that the owner had gone out of her way to serve them overshadowed any possible reason to complain.

When the group started out, the sun's rising was still not strong enough to burn through the dense fog.

At first, the paved road was easily passable, but it soon narrowed and pavement was replaced by dirt. They moved into an overgrown forest. The farther they went, the more difficult the trail became. The lushness of the forest dimmed against tall, massive, gray slates of barren rock as they made their way up the path. The three groups formed and over time separated.

Cautiously moving at their own pace, each group made their way up the slippery rock path. Occasionally a lone bush or tree could be seen through the fog.

Honey, Jocelyn, and Ada were the first to arrive at an unusual-looking barren tree. A large flock of buzzards, maybe hundreds, were perched on its large branches bending them so low it looked as if they were about to break. Without warning, the buzzards simultaneously flew off. The sounds of their calls were soft and eerie.

Honey stared off into the distance at a barely visible, narrow ledge on a cliff they would have to cross. It appeared to her to be the perfect spot for a mishap.

When they reached the palisade, Honey slowed her pace. Jocelyn looked back over her shoulder, "Something wrong?"

"My ankle is bothering me. I'm going to slow down a little. I don't want to risk injuring it further. I won't be far behind. Don't slow down on my account."

As expected, Jocelyn and Ada did not slow down. Honey watched them continue onward and disappear in the fog. She waited for Amanda and Rachael under the cover of the thick fog.

Little time passed before Amanda and Rachael reached Honey.

"Taking a break?" Rachael asked.

"Yeah," Honey answered.

"Where's Jocelyn and Ada?" Amanda asked.

"They're just a short distance ahead, but this fog is so thick you can't see much more than an arm's length ahead. Occasionally I've gotten a glimpse of the cliffs up above us. With this ankle I've come close to losing my footing a few times already." Realizing she was talking more than usual due to nervousness, she lowered her voice, adding, "I just need to go slow."

Amanda and Rachael walked with Honey. Between the fog and maneuvering over slippery rocks, the climb to the ledge took longer than Honey expected.

Once they were on the ledge, Honey noted the spot was better than expected. The ledge was so narrow they would have to cross single file. All she needed to do was to convince Rachael to lead the way.

"Rachael, would you mind scouting ahead and let me know what to expect? My leg is really stiff," Honey asked.

"Not at all," Rachael answered.

Honey gave Rachael a few minutes to get ahead. Honey closed her hiking poles and put them into her pack to give her better flexibility to shove Amanda off the cliff. Then she suggested, "Amanda, if you go slower I can follow you."

"Sure thing."

Honey followed close behind. She soon saw her chance, and quickly moved up behind Amanda. However, when she leaned forward to push her, a goat suddenly emerged from out of the fog. A rock broke loose under Honey's foot. She lost her footing and started to fall. Inside her head, she heard herself screaming. Her world had stopped. Tumbling down the side of the cliff she grabbed a bush. She knew her legs and arms were bruised, yet fear and shock outweighed the pain. She pushed her leg into a crevice in the rock.

Amanda turned, dropped her poles down, and lay on the ground to reach for Honey. Her reach was sufficient to grab Honey's free arm. Yet, the pack on Amanda's back did not allow the leverage she needed, nor did she have the strength to pull Honey up. Amanda screamed for help, and held onto Honey's arm as best she could. "Honey, hold on."

Rachael heard the screams for help and within minutes was helping Amanda. Rachael grabbed Honey's arm that was held by Amanda.

"Amanda, get your pack off then grab her other arm. Together we can pull her up."

Amanda whipped off her backpack, and between the two of them, they were able to pull Honey back onto the ledge.

After sitting for a few minutes, Honey tried to stand, but putting weight on the leg elicited pain.

Amanda noticed the painful look on Honey's face. "Your ankle is really swollen. We need to wrap it so you can continue."

Rachael picked up Honey's backpack, and asked, "Did you lose your poles?"

"No, they're inside my pack."

Rachael shrugged her shoulders and looked at Amanda as if to say, *How stupid was that?*

Rachael used her bandana, Amanda's scarf and two small tree branches to create a splint for Honey's leg.

When the splint was secure, Honey leaned forward to pick up her backpack. Rachael noticed a painful grimace on Honey's face and stopped her. "Look, you're not going to make it down the other side with that weight on your back. Amanda and I will take turns carrying your backpack."

Confusion and rage raced through Honey's mind. She had failed again, and worse, she owed these girls her life.

Due to the slow pace the girls now traveled, Faith and Tina caught up with them near Aviles.

Seeing Honey limping and Amanda carrying Honey's backpack, Faith asked, "What happened?"

"It was awful, Mom. There was this goat, a rock broke loose, and Honey slipped off that cliff. You know the one where we had to go single file. Luckily, she caught the branch of a tree and held on until Rachael and I could pull her up."

"I was never so scared in my life, as when we went over that pass," Tina said.

With Honey traveling slowly due to her injury, the five walked together.

"I'd be happy to take a turn carrying Honey's pack," Faith offered.

With all this noble attention, Honey found her nerves becoming more and more frazzled as the day wore on.

At the bottom of a ravine, they came to a stream. The clear water rippled over the rocks.

"Honey, let's take a break. You can soak your ankle in the cool water. It might help reduce some of the swelling," Faith suggested.

The nicer the girls were to her, the angrier Honey felt.

After a short break, on their way to Aviles, Honey fumed, gnashed her teeth quietly to hide her frustration, while the others marveled at the sights of medieval homes and glorious gardens.

"Honey, things will get better. Try not to think so much. Tomorrow is a rest day. You'll have a whole day to take care of your ankle," Faith said.

Still upset, Honey changed the topic of conversation. "Faith, nothing seems to get you down. What's your secret?"

"Oh, looks can be deceiving, but mostly, I do okay. A couple of years ago, I thought my life couldn't get any worse. I was raised where good family relations were the key to life's success. I had failed miserably in that arena. My husband was abusive, and my daughter and I were at odds with each other. I was a mess."

"Things seem okay between you two now," Honey said.

"Better for sure. It's a long story."

Honey wanted desperately to hear Faith's story. She knew she'd catch her in a lie. "Hey, if it's something you don't want to talk about, that's fine. But, listening to a story right now might help keep my mind off the pain in this ankle."

"The fact is. I was angry at the world. I was even jealous of Tina's happy family life. Her husband was loving and supportive. Her son and daughter were devoted to family. Luckily, my mother was very supportive. She suggested I go to a sweat lodge and turn to meditation and the Great Spirit for help."

"I gather your mother is Native American," Honey said.

"Yes. I did as she suggested and found the peace I was looking for."

Honey thought, *What a bunch of bull. She kills her ex-husband and acts like she's holier-than-thou.*

Their arrival in Aviles was as depressing to Honey as it was exhilarating to the others. The town was clean, quaint, and friendly. When they approached the place where they would spend a day of rest, everyone was joyful except Honey.

A garden area was visible through double glass doors when they entered their hotel. "Look at those gardens in the back. How great is this? We're staying in an old palace." Rachael said.

After getting settled in, keeping her ankle iced, and a good short rest, Honey reclaimed her composure. In an attempt to give her ankle plenty of time to rest she used her hiking poles as crutches and limped her way to a bench in the rose garden. She forced all thoughts of how Amanda had saved her life out of her mind. She still had the poison. She would let her ankle heal a few days then finish the deed.

Spanish Dancers

27

REFLECTIONS

Four days had passed since their last rest day. The day's had been challenging, but thoughts of another rest day in Ribadeo gave everyone the strength they needed to conquer the day.

Honey sat with Jocelyn and Ada on the Ribadeo Bridge taking a final rest break before heading into town. Jocelyn stood to leave.

"I'm going to sit here a little longer. I can see Ribadeo from here and I'd like to take a few pictures from this vantage point. I'll catch up with you later," Honey said.

The view in front of Honey was postcard perfect. White buildings with red-tiled roofs were staggered in a mosaic pattern. This was the last village where they would see the sea. From this point they would turn inland to Santiago.

Honey turned toward the sun, allowing its warmth to soothe her troubled mind. She closed her eyes and reflected on their journey from Aviles to Ribadeo.

These last few days had taken over hills through farmlands and backyards of private homes. There had been no opportunities for any "mishaps" while hiking on private property. She couldn't tell if anyone was home and watching. She was running out of time to finish the job.

It was late in the day when Faith, Tina, Amanda, and Rachael reached the Ribadeo Bridge. They too stopped to rest and admire the view before heading into town. For Faith the last four days had passed slowly. The day's had been long, and when the sun was about to set she was so afraid they wouldn't make it into town before dark.

Faith stood, Are you girls ready to head to town?"

Tina answered, "Yeah. I know we've passed through some glorious lands, but everything has become a blur."

Faith smiled reassuringly. "I'm sure you haven't forgotten our singing in the town's square with Amanda and Rachael in Cadavedo, or the nice fellow who escorted us through Luarca and took us to the tourist center so we could get our *Camino* passports stamped."

"I tell you what surprised me the most. I don't remember where we were, but going through all those mountains that were being clear-cut was disturbing. It was scary how the soil eroded under our feet," Rachael said.

"Not to change the subject. I know you get upset every time I talk about taking a day off, but hold your breath. Don't say anything for a minute. I want to take an extra day to rest after Ribadeo. I need the break. We're getting close to the French route and I don't want to miss any of those days, and you need to spend time with Amanda before this trip ends," Tina said.

Amanda, who had been walking along side Faith, took her mother's hand and whispered, "Mom, you can discuss it later. She's changed her mind before, after she gets a chance to rest."

It was dusk when they came to the sea. There they checked into a marvelous hotel overlooking magnificent tall cliffs and the sea.

"Tina, look at the people walking along the tops of those cliffs," Amanda said.

"If you're suggesting we add that to our day's adventure, you can count me out. See the people sitting on the beach in that cove area? That's for me," Tina said.

"How does 8:00 p.m. sound for meeting for dinner?" Faith asked.

"Sounds good to me," Rachael said.

"Me too," Amanda answered.

After a long, rejuvenating shower, while Tina was getting ready for dinner, Faith took a short stroll out onto the hotel's decking which overlooked the sea. The last rays from the setting sun blasted an array of pinks, reds, and purples through the sky. Faith sighed contently, *Just beautiful.*

Honey had been enjoying the spectacular view as well. Seeing Honey, Faith joined her on the deck, and asked, "It's an amazing sight, isn't it?"

"It is. Are you eating at the hotel or venturing out this evening?

"We're eating here. Meeting at 8:00 p.m. You're welcome to join us. The others too, if they'd like."

"I'd like to. I'll check with the others."

Together they stood silently watching the sun hide behind the earth. Finally, Honey turned to leave, "I'll check with the others. We may see you at dinner."

The entire group met for dinner.

Salmon was the meal of choice. Praises for the meal and accommodations took precedent over any misgiving they had for the last few days.

After eating, they went to their rooms. As Faith climbed into her comfortable bed, the sound of waves rolling into shore entered their window lulling her into a pleasant sleep.

Down the hall, Honey listened to the roar of the ocean, but sleep did not come easily. She reviewed her plan over and over again.

28

RIBADEO

It was a good day to rest. Everyone slept in, and arrived at almost the same time for breakfast outside on the hotel veranda.

After several discussions regarding possibilities for the day, Faith, Amanda, and Rachael decided to check out the Fort of San Damian. Jocelyn, Honey, and Ada decided to shop, and Tina announced she was going to the beach with a good book.

Before the group went their separate ways, Ada asked, "Shall we meet later for dinner? The hotel's restaurant was wonderful, but do we want to try somewhere else in town tonight?"

"I'm up for anything," Tina said.

"I'd like to try a local restaurant. I'll check at the front desk, and leave word where we'll be. I'll shoot for an 8:00 p.m. dinner time," Jocelyn said.

Each enjoyed their day in their own way, and when they met for dinner, all were present except Amanda and Rachael.

Faith shrugged her shoulders as she looked at the others at the table. "They left word for us to go on without them. They said they'd join us. But please, go ahead and order."

The group finished ordering and still the girls had not arrived.

"Do you think they're coming?" Tina asked.

Just then, Amanda and Rachael entered the restaurant. Their energy bubbled with enthusiasm as they came to the table.

"Wasn't the Fort of San Damian amazing? And the shops were fabulous," Rachael said.

Faith noticed a mischievous look on Amanda's face. Amanda smiled. "Look what I found." She held a *Camino* shell necklace. It had the word *'Camino'* and a red cross painted on it. "I've been looking for this type of shell since we started our trip. We must be getting close to Santiago since I was finally able to find one."

While the women admired her necklace, Rachael and Amanda both tapped their feet excitedly. Then they pulled their hands from behind their backs and held out necklaces for each of the other women. Each accepted their gift enthusiastically, except Jocelyn. "I found one of these yesterday. You keep this one in case someone misplaces theirs. Thanks just the same."

After dinner, when Faith climbed into her comfortable bed, she thought, *This has been one of the most pleasant days of the trip. Tomorrow we begin our turn inland toward Santiago and away from the sea. We are past the half-way mark. The only thing that could make it better is if Tina says she is walking tomorrow.*

At that moment, as if Tina had heard Faith's thoughts, she said, "I feel pretty good. I think I'm going to walk tomorrow."

29

RIBADEO TO LOURENZA

The recent rains accompanied by fierce winds from Ribadeo to Lourenza had filled the countryside with debris. The path took them into and out of dense forests where prickly-pear undergrowth scattered amongst the foliage tore at their clothes and ankles. Often without warning, the group would make a turn and find an unexpected abrupt climb. The descents were steeper than in weeks past, and laden with uprooted trees from the heavy winds.

Climbing over fallen trees, they encountered tree roots that formed unnatural ramparts. Scaling fallen tree branches or moving them off the path became the norm for the day. It frequently took half an hour for Tina to remove her backpack, toss it to Faith, and then climb over the fat logs.

At one point, scaling over a large tree stump caused Tina to loose her balance and slip downward. Before hitting the ground, she caught a limb and held it tight to prevent a fall. Eventually she made it over the tree stump safely and was back on the path, but her hand, arms and legs were covered with cuts.

Frustrated Tina announced. "Jocelyn told me it would get harder when we moved away from the sea. This is not for me."

Hearing the frustration in Tina's voice, Faith sat down on a log. "Tina, you've been doing great. Do you think this is easy for any of us? I don't want to finish this trip without you by my side. We're only 75 miles from Santiago. Don't quit on me now."

Tina acquiesced to Faith's pleading. "Okay. Stop your blubbering, and let's get this show on the road."

Their arrival in Lourenza was late, after 10:30 p.m., two hours after the rest had eaten and gone to their rooms. Fortunately, the hotel, The Union, was still serving dinner. Faith's spirits were uplifted when Amanda entered the restaurant giving her a warm greeting and hug. Exhausted, Tina and Faith dined and then went to their room.

30

LOURENZA TO ABADIN

Mid-morning the following day, still drained from the previous day's hike, Tina and Faith found they were falling far behind the others. They came to an open meadow where a white farm house with a red-tiled roof and a white picket fence caught Faith's attention. A colorful garden and a freshly-painted red barn added to the grandeur of this spectacular sight. Faith thought the view was picture postcard. Then, a gate in the fence was pushed open by a small black-and-white sheep dog. At first, he directed the sheep behind the fence through the gate and let them go wherever they wanted. Then, the dog circled his flock persuading them to head to the grassy meadow in front of them. As if putting on a show for Faith and Tina, he rounded up his flock and led them back inside the fenced area, and closed the gate.

"I could swear that dog is smiling at us," Faith said.

"I know. Wasn't that great? I think he was showing off."

Later in the day as they continued on their trek, the path leveled. At first, they were grateful for the easier walk, until . . .

"My eyes are burning. What is that stench?" Tina asked while picking up her pace. "Let's get pass this, whatever it is." The two looked down the slope of the mountain. "I've never seen so many small long shacks. They're covering this whole side of the mountain. It's daytime and I can see lights are on inside them."

"They're chicken coops."

"Boy, I had no idea they could stink like this."

"So, now I know how to get you to move faster. Put something smelly in your path and you're out of there," Faith laughed.

Holding her nose, Tina chuckled. "Well, I remember that day when we were training, and that good-looking fellow came along. You sure did run fast to catch up with him. So to get us moving faster, it's a good-looking male's butt for you and a stinky chicken coop for me.

On the path to Abadin, after Honey, Jocelyn, and Ada crested the top of the mountain, the landscape changed and once again became heavily treed.

Ada stopped to adjust her backpack. "I hope this is the last of these downed trees we have to climb over today. I've torn my pants and shirt getting over and around these exposed roots and trunks."

When Jocelyn and Ada started off down the hill, lost in thought, Honey didn't notice their departure.

"You coming?" Jocelyn called out.

"Yeah," Honey answered, shifting her feet uncomfortably.

Honey's body tensed in rebellion. Her gaze hardened. Hesitantly, she took her place at the end of the line. Her feet and back ached. She noticed Jocelyn take a pain pill, and Ada was walking with a limp in her step. Yet, in spite of their obvious discomfort, their pace remained constant even as their postures continued to stiffen. The way they were marching along reminded Honey of her father. Her father walked like that on the day he took her and her sister to town to buy his booze. He always drank a lot, but that evening he drank more than usual. Honey had seen an empty bottle of Jack Daniels on the floor, and another one beside him on the coffee table. There was no telling if there were more. He yelled at her sister to fix dinner. She could tell by the look in her sister's eyes and by the tone of her father's voice that he would hurt them before the night was over. Usually, Margie urged her to hide in a closet or under the bed. She always took the brunt of his abuse to protect her.

Later that evening when the door to her room opened, she couldn't breathe.

She was happy when she realized it was Margie. Only this night Margie's eyes seemed void of life. Honey had seen her beaten up before, but never had she seen that look in her eyes.

They snuck out. Margie took her to the storm cellar, opened the cellar's door, and told her to find a box, hide in it, and not to come out until she came for her.

She did as instructed. Two days she waited before the cellar door opened. She waited for Margie to call her name.

Instead, a uniformed man opened the box she was hiding in. She was told her sister was dead, that her father had killed her. That was day her childhood ended.

Deep in thought, Honey's pace slowed. When she became aware of it, she accelerated to catch up with Jocelyn and Ada. As she did, anger replaced sadness.

31

ABADIN TO VILALBA

All morning and into the late afternoon the thick foreboding fog never lifted. Bad weather forced all three groups to alternately pull out and then put away their rain ponchos. Severe climbs required them to navigate around deep mud-holes filled with waters. Despite this, Tina endured it without complaint.

They crossed an old stone bridge and came to an area where dozens of beautiful castles came partially into view.

"Faith, look! Are they abandoned? Let's take that path to get closer."

When they came to a field where they could see the castles clearly, Faith said, "I wonder what happened to make people leave those beautiful homes?"

Tina's voice was solemn. "Obviously, something happened where they couldn't afford the upkeep. We've heard many villagers complain that their children have moved to larger cities to find employment. I wish I could afford to buy one and fix it up."

"Me too. Guess we'll have to buy a lottery ticket when we get home."

The rest of the day they laughed at the challenges and reflected on their blessings.

Sounds of civilization could be heard as they neared Vilalba, a small town nestled deep in a valley.

Contentedly, Tina reported, "We're arriving early enough today to have a few minutes to rest before dinner."

Faith smiled, and gave her friend a supportive nod.

Tired but content in their day's achievement, they arrived happily in Vilalba.

32

VILALBA

On rest days, activities for Rachael and Amanda rarely began before 10:00 a.m., and today would be no exception. At 10:30 Amanda knocked on her mother's door. She had heard them moving around in their room and knew they were up.

"Have you had breakfast yet?" Amanda asked.

"Just coffee. We thought we'd wait for you two. And by now it would probably be more proper to say we're off to enjoy brunch," Faith answered.

The cobblestone streets of Vilalba depicted its medieval heritage, and stone buildings graced narrow streets. As they walked, the aroma of freshly-brewed coffee pulled them into a family-owned restaurant. The tables were covered with red-and-green plaid tablecloths. Three children, ranging from what Faith guessed were four to ten years of age helped their mother set the tables with sugar jars, and salt and pepper shakers.

Their mother smiled, greeted them with a warm "*Buenos Dias,*" and directed them to a table.

While enjoying egg tapas, fresh pastries, and cappuccinos, the four recounted and laughed about their last few days' ordeals.

"Isn't it amazing how one day's suffering becomes material for jokes the following day," Rachael said.

"That may be true for you, but I think it's going to take more than a few days before I see this trip in a humorous light," Tina said.

Caffeinated and with full bellies they left the restaurant and walked to the small, well-maintained church of Santa Maria.

After touring the church, they went next door to visit the Parador Nacional Hotel. They strolled through the 15th century structure, admiring the architectural conversion from castle to hotel. Amanda noticed tapestries on the wall. "Aren't they magnificent? The colors are so vibrant. I love the rich red, purple, and gold threads. By the way, there's a museum not far from here. I picked up this book at a book shop a couple of towns ago. It mentions hill-forts nearby of megalithic design. Want to know what megalithic means?" Rachael asked.

"Go ahead. Dazzle us with your information," Tina said.

"Megalithic structures are made of large interlocking stones, without using mortar or cement. We passed a few bridges along the way that looked megalithic," Rachael said.

"Say that word one more time and I'm going to throw something at you," Tina joked.

"The book says primitive stone tools and other pre-historic artifacts that were found in this area are on display in the town's museum. The museum was converted from an old municipal prison. Must be crime has gone down in this area. Want to go?" Rachael asked.

"I'd rather rest, so later I'm not too tired to enjoy a good meal with you. But if you go by a shop that sells San Simon cheese, I'd love some. If we can ship it home, let me know," Tina said.

"I'm gathering this is the cheese of the area. What's so special about San Simon cheese?" Faith asked.

"They make it in the shape of a spinning wheel, and it's smoked. I've heard it's fabulous."

Tina returned to the hotel to rest while Faith, Rachael, and Amanda took in more of Vilalba's sights. Four hours later, they returned to the hotel to rest. Finding Tina sound asleep, Faith picked up a book, but before she finished two pages, she too was dozing.

That evening Faith, Tina, Amanda, and Rachael joined the others for dinner. As soon as Tina took her seat, Jocelyn said. "At least on rest days, you two can make it to dinner."

Rachael's jaw tightened. She interrupted Jocelyn before she could say more. "Did you know that this town connects to another *Camino* path called the *A Coruna?* The brochure I read said, years past, pirates and thieves would rob pilgrims on their journey, so the pilgrims created different ways to avoid them. It also mentioned criminals were sometimes released to walk the path for penance. They were sent out with balls and chains still on their legs. These prisoners had to depend on the generosity of others to feed them along the way. If they made it to Santiago, some would be freed."

"Rachael, thanks to you, I'll return home having learned some really interesting facts about this country and its people," Faith said.

Tina lifted her glass of wine. "I'm not sure what I would have eaten without your interpreting the menus. I'd like to make a toast to Jocelyn for finding some of the loveliest places to stay, and to Rachael for saving us at meals."

The group toasted, and during the rest of the meal, conversations remained pleasant.

That evening back in their room, Tina asked, "Why do you think our walking slower upsets Jocelyn?"

"I think it's a matter of her being out of control. When we're not with them, she doesn't have control over us, and she thinks of this trip as her show. And in some ways it is. She did most of the planning. All I can say is, each of us is here to learn, and to take home from this trip what we need. Maybe our presence is actually helping Jocelyn in some way we can't see," Faith said.

"So why doesn't she get upset when Amanda and Rachael don't stay with them?" Tina asked.

"Probably because she discounts teenagers," Then in a more serious tone, Faith added, "Anyway, it's not worth worrying about. Let's work on enjoying these last few days. Tomorrow looks like it will be a sunny, cool day. There's a saying that helps me when I encounter a situation where my intent is good, but someone feels otherwise: 'It's never about me and them. It's only about me and God.'"

33

VILALBA TO BAAMONDE

The hike from Vilalba to Baamonde was much easier than previous days. At several points along the way, Rachael and Amanda caught up and hiked with Jocelyn, Ada, and Honey. The path took them over medieval bridges, and into a small town where the group, minus Faith and Tina, enjoyed a pleasant lunch in a courtyard filled with brightly colored flowers. Honey sat next to Amanda. "It looks like today may not be so bad. Guess that means you girls will be out on the town this evening."

"If the day doesn't change or get tougher, we might, but I'm not making any quick judgments. I've been caught off-guard too many times. I don't even want to think about how often I believed we were almost to our destination, only to find out we still had miles to go," Amanda said.

"Good point," Honey said.

"Not to burst any bubbles here, but the accommodations for this evening could be a little rough. We're staying in a hostel connected to a truck stop. I'm not even sure we will be near a town," Jocelyn said.

Before the group finished lunch, Faith and Tina arrived at the restaurant. When Jocelyn, Ada, and Honey stood to leave, Amanda said, "We're going to hang out here with Mom and Tina for awhile. See you later."

Amanda and Rachael trekked with Tina and Faith the rest of the day. By late afternoon, they came to a deserted highway. In the distance, they saw the truck stop. It stood like an oasis in a desert.

When they reached the truck stop, Jocelyn, Ada, and Honey were already sitting out front.

"We're waiting for someone to show up and let us in the building next door. It's locked," Jocelyn said.

"At least the truck stop isn't adding more steps to our day. This reminds me of when Mom was trying to get to the Smokey Mountains and we got lost on the Blue Ridge Parkway. The only life we found was at a truck stop." Amanda said.

Laborers and tradesmen sat nearby in old metal chairs, smoking and drinking.

As the group walked to the entrance and passed by the men, an older gap-toothed gentleman smiled and in Spanish, commented on the girls' beauty, then wished them a pleasant evening.

Another man rose from his chair and offered to escort them to the station where they would be able to pick up the key. As the group followed this man, a young woman walked toward them with a key in her hand.

Amanda watched the young woman fling aside the men's suggestive comments as she passed them, and came to open the door.

"*Senorita, muchas gracias,*" Amanda greeted the woman.

Rachael smiled while her hands gestured delight in her coming to their rescue. "*Hola. Hablas Ingles? Como se llama usted?*"

"*Si,* I speak *Ingles* well. *Me* name *es* Maria. I can open the building for you."

"*Muchas gracias,* Maria. Is there a good place to have dinner nearby, within walking distance?"

Maria waved her arms excitedly, while in charming broken English, she answered. "*Si,* We have a wonderful restaurant, and you are so lucky. Victor Correl Castro, a well-known sculptor is in town. He is internationally acclaimed. His brother owns the restaurant. The restaurant is *muy bien.* It's not far from here, and Victor will be there tonight. You can even see some of Castro's carvings in the trees on your way to the restaurant. They are amazing." Maria gave Rachael directions to the restaurant.

"*Muchos gracias.*" Rachael said.

Amanda waved. "*Adios,* Maria. *Mucho gusto.*"

After climbing four flights of stairs to get to their room, to their surprise, they found their luggage already there on the floor.

"Amazing isn't it? I wonder when and who brought our luggage to our room. That was really nice. We should find out who did this for us, and give him a tip. Lugging those bags up here couldn't have been fun," Amanda said.

Later that evening, all seven walked together to the restaurant. They took a detour to see Victor Castro's tree carvings.

Rachael was the first to spot the sculptures carved inside one of the trees. "This is amazing."

After finding two more sculptures, they made their way to the restaurant.

Inside, they found the tables were too small for them to sit together. Amanda, Faith, Rachael, and Tina sat at one table while Jocelyn, Honey, and Ada sat at another.

The presence of two attractive girls, Amanda and Rachael, brought out the best in the owner. He flirted with the girls, and spun tales for them. When his brother, Victor Castro overheard the commotion, he made a dashing appearance. The entire group spent time complimenting the artist. Faith, Tina, Amanda, and Rachael remained long after the others returned to the truck stop, socializing with the brothers and townsfolk.

Back at the truck stop in her room, Honey pretended to sleep while listening for Amanda and Rachael's return.

Honey did her best to stay awake. But time got away from her. She read, ate chocolates, and wrote in her journal, but she waited for their return so long she drifted off to the world of sleep and nightmares. When she awoke the following morning, not only was she distraught over having fallen asleep, but she found herself haunted by a vivid dream. She was walking with Amanda. They were alone. As they stood before a large stone crucifix of the body of Christ carved in a three-dimensional form she pulled out her syringe. When she moved toward Amanda to complete the deed, her sister Margie stepped out from behind the crucifix. She held up her hand, gesturing for her to stop. "Honey, no. Don't do it. Remember, we're good girls." It all seemed too real.

Ada turned over in bed. "Honey, did you hear something in our room last night? I could have sworn I heard a voice."

Honey's hands trembled. "No, it must have been the wind."

34

BAAMONDE TO SOBRADO DOS MONXES

Every day during this final week heading to Santiago, more and more pilgrims appeared on the path.

Meeting pilgrims from other parts of the world added excitement to the day's hike into Sobrado dos Monxes. Jocelyn, Ada, Honey, Amanda, and Rachael stopped frequently during the day to visit with other pilgrims. Stopping so often meant Faith and Tina were never far behind, and several times during the day were even able to catch up.

At one point, when Ada glanced back she noticed a gray-haired Spanish couple coming up the trail a short distance behind them. "They must be twice our age, and yet they are walking faster than we are. They're going to pass us again. I hope to be in as good a shape as they are when I get to be their age."

"Me, too," Honey said as she looked back over her shoulder, and waved to the couple. A close distance behind the Spanish couple, Honey saw Amanda and Rachael coming up the trail. Four good-looking college boys kept pace with the girls. The group conversed non-stop. The boys were keeping the girls happily entertained. Looking away, Honey thought, *The police will think they partied with the wrong group. Killing her the night before we head into Santiago will make up for all my failed attempts along the way.*

Coming into the city, Jocelyn remarked, "There must be some sort of festival going on here today. I haven't seen this many people since Bilbao. We should stop for something to eat before searching for our lodging."

While they sat in the restaurant, Honey saw Amanda and Rachael pass by. Their male entourage had obviously moved on. It was just the two of them.

"Should I catch them and let them know we're here?" Honey asked.

Jocelyn shrugged her shoulders. "Sure, why not?"

Honey stepped outside of the restaurant to call to the girls. "We're in here."

The two turned and followed Honey into the restaurant. "Isn't this the most glorious day? The sun's shining, the weather's cool, and there's a festival going on. There are going to be bands playing and there will be dancing in the square this evening," Rachael said.

"Should have figured you girls would have already checked out the festivities," Ada responded.

"I hope our hotel isn't too far out of town. I'd like to get cleaned up and come back later," Rachael said.

Jocelyn felt she needed to clarify the lodging plans, and spoke up. "We're not in a hotel this evening. I believe we'll be staying in a bed-and-breakfast a good distance away from town."

"Guess we'll do some sightseeing now, just in case it's too far to return to town later," Amanda said.

When they finished lunch, Honey asked Amanda, "We're heading over to the Abbey. Want to join us?"

"Not right now. We're going to wait for Tina and Mom. Probably do some window shopping while we wait for them to catch up. See you later."

Amanda and Rachael stopped in a few shops, but didn't try on clothes since they were too dirty. They came to a bakery. "Amanda, you know what I love best about this trip?" Rachael asked.

"No, what?"

"The fact that we can eat anything we like no matter how fattening and still lose weight. I haven't checked how much I've lost, but I had to buy a belt to hold up these pants. You look like you've lost quite a bit of weight, too."

"I have, just not sure how much."

Glancing down the street, Amanda spied Tina and her mother coming towards them. "It's hard to miss those two, especially with my Mom's hair in those braids, and Tina's big floppy walking hat. You check out the delights while I wait outside for them."

When Tina saw Amanda, she asked, "Did you girls eat already?"

"We did, but we were just about to order dessert before we go check out the Abbey. Why don't you just get a snack to hold you off so we can go to the Abbey together? The desserts look fabulous. The restaurants will still be open later and you can get a real meal before hiking to wherever we are staying," Amanda said.

"Dessert before lunch? Sounds okay to me. How about you, Tina?" Faith asked.

"I'm game. Plus, it smells divine in there."

Amanda and Faith chose different chocolate temptations, and Tina and Rachael picked out cream-filled pastries.

"Think this will be enough for us to share?" Amanda asked.

Tina, feeling good about the freedom to eat answered, "If not, we'll simply buy more. I don't know how I will ever survive when I get back home. Eating anything without worrying or thinking has been a joy. But now that I've lost so much weight, I don't want to rebound after I get home."

"Let's not brood about it now. Let's just enjoy the moment," Faith said.

Jocelyn, Honey, and Ada were leaving the Abbey when Faith's group arrived. Rachael went to Jocelyn. "How was it?"

"Old and run down," Jocelyn answered as if bored to death, then continued, "We're going to head home for the night. You can come along. There's not much to see."

We'll see for ourselves, Tina thought, but remarked in a pleasant tone, "We're here so we might as well check it out. See you later."

A few minutes later in the Abbey, Rachael resumed her role as tour guide. She read, "The large Cistercian Monastery was built in the 12th Century by the Benedictines. It was remodeled in the 17th Century, and abandoned in the 18th Century after authorities closed the Abbey. It's so big. Maybe there just weren't enough people to support it. In 1954, a plan was put into effect to restore a portion of it."

A monk entered the cathedral. "Please feel free to walk around."

Rachael answered for the group. "Thank you."

As they walked through the abandoned cathedral, Amanda said, "This is so eerie. Imagine how grand this place must have been! You can still see remnants of frescos on the walls."

Rachael added, "Did you know that monks made copies of many frescos in mosaic works of art? These mosaics were created matching the original fresco colors and are used today to match the original colors during restorations since so many frescos have faded over time."

"Is there anything you don't know about these churches?" Amanda asked.

"I still have a lot to learn."

From across the room, Rachael and Amanda heard Faith call out. "Look, there's a replica of this building on the table in the corner." But when the girls approached, Rachael spoke up. "It isn't this church. It's an exact replica of the Cathedral De Santiago."

"I'm getting chills," Amanda said.

Knowing they would soon arrive in Santiago, the four examined the structure, mesmerized by its workmanship.

The group worked their way to the chapel and kitchen areas of the Abbey.

As they left the chapel Rachael said. "We're thinking of heading on to our hotel so we can get cleaned up and return for the evening festivities."

"This town is so nice. We might still be here when you return. Once I get to where we're staying the night, I won't want to come back," Faith said.

"And I want to get something to eat before we start back." Tina added.

As Amanda and Rachael started off down the road, Amanda smiled. "Have fun."

Faith and Tina found a quaint restaurant with outdoor café seating.

Tina read the menu. "They've got hamburgers."

"Somehow, I don't think they're going to be like American hamburgers, but I'll try one," Faith said.

Both agreed to try the hamburger meals. Soon their meals arrived with two bottles of wine.

"Certainly doesn't look like any *Happy Meal* from McDonald's, does it?" Tina asked.

"Not one bit, but the meat does look like hamburger. It even looks delicious."

Faith poured a glass of wine for each of them. "We may have to sleep on a park bench. We're going to be too relaxed to walk the rest of the way."

Faith paused and carefully chose her words before asking. "Tina, are you happy you made the trip?"

"I am. You know how angry I was at Jimmy for getting sick and at God for letting this happen to him. Being a young widow wasn't how I saw my life. I don't want to be alone."

"But Tina, he isn't dead yet. And you're always angry and yelling at him. You're wasting your last days with him. You think he wants to die and leave you and your children?"

"I know you're right, and when I get home, I plan on changing that. I'm going to meditate, and be more patient with him."

Faith smiled. "Be more patient with yourself as well. Okay?"

For several hours, Faith and Tina enjoyed the town. At dusk, they meandered to their night's accommodations.

The road to their bed-and-breakfast turned out to be a very pleasant walk, with level ground and obstacle free. When they arrived, they found Jocelyn, Ada, and Honey lounging in the living room.

"It's almost time for dinner. The owner said she will be serving at eight," Ada said.

"We'll be ready, but we ate a late lunch so we won't be too hungry. But I'd never turn down a home-cooked meal. By the way, we didn't pass the girls on our way in. Are they around?" Faith asked.

"They're getting dressed. They plan to walk back to town in the dark for the fiesta. I told them they're crazy. But I guess that's your job, Mom," Jocelyn said.

"They're not kids. If that's what they want to do, it's up to them."

Amanda and Rachael entered the room just in time to hear Jocelyn's comment and Faith's response.

Faith looked directly at her daughter, smiled and continued, "As crazy as I think that idea is."

Amanda and Rachael smiled. "Don't worry Mom. We've got flashlights. You saw the road is really good from here to town. We won't be late."

"Now, that's funny. There is no way you're not going to be late when dinner's at 8:00 p.m. By the way, did you find out what the town is celebrating?"

"Of course we did," Rachael answered. "A well-known popular Spanish band is in town to give a concert. One of the band members is from this town, so the entire town is turning out to hear them. There will be dancing, singing, and food. Sounds great, doesn't it?"

"Too much for me, but have a great time," Faith said.

"That goes double for me," Tina added.

That goes triple for me, thought Honey, *for this is the last night of your life, Amanda. Enjoy it well.*

35

SOBRADO DOS MONXES TO ARZUA

The following day, with less than three hours of sleep, Amanda and Rachael had no problems walking at a slower pace with Faith and Tina. Besides the enchanting scenery, the people they met along the way were pleasant and entertaining. They met two women from Paris, a foursome from Japan, and an Irish lass traveling alone.

Faith leaned in close to Tina and whispered, "Now that the *Northern Route* has met the *French Route* we are running into so many young people on the path. I bet Amanda and Rachael wish we had taken the *French route* instead of the *Northern route.*"

Faith looked up and saw Amanda and Rachael waiting for them by a medieval bridge. "Their ears must have been burning. They must have heard me talking about them."

"Maybe, but they certainly aren't bored now, and I really doubt that those two ever were," Tina sighed and continued, "I can't believe tomorrow is our last day before we arrive in Santiago. A few weeks ago, I thought this day would never come. Now, it seems as if this adventure only began a few days ago," Tina said.

When Faith and Tina saw their hotel, they were pleased to find it was located directly on the path, and even more pleased to discover it had a restaurant.

Inside the hotel lobby, backpacks were stacked against every wall and chair. People of various ethnicities and ages sat on chairs or on the floor sharing stories of their *Camino* adventures.

"Did you ever think we'd see so many people on the path?" Rachael asked.

"Not really," Tina answered.

After they registered, Faith asked. "What time should we meet for dinner?"

"Mom, we met some really nice kids along the way today. We said we'd hook up for dinner. Would you be upset if we skipped out on you tonight? I haven't seen the others, so I don't know what they have planned."

"Go have fun with your friends. Meeting people your age from other countries isn't an everyday occurrence. It's an experience not to miss. Have fun."

Shortly after Amanda and Rachael left to join their newly-acquired friends, the Spanish couple, John and Maria entered the lobby, seeing Faith and Tina the couple approached and invited them to dinner. Faith and Tina graciously accepted.

At dinner, Faith found the couple adorable. John asked questions about American politics. Maria inquired about vacation spots in the U.S. Tina and Faith asked the couple similar questions about Spain. Each enjoyed learning about the others' culture while they ate their meals.

"I've got to ask. I haven't seen many Spaniards on the trail. Why not?" Faith asked.

Maria laughed, "I guess it's because we look so tired and dirty coming off the trails."

With a smile, Faith nodded understandingly.

When they finished dinner, Faith and Tina bid their goodbyes.

Maria smiled, "We'll probably see you on the road tomorrow or in Santiago. I'm so excited."

Faith answered for herself and Tina, "Us too!"

Leaving the restaurant, Tina turned to Faith. "I'm going to see if there's a phone I can use to call home. I want to talk to Jimmy."

"If you find one, I'd like to call home, too."

At the front desk, Tina was told, "Some rooms have phones and others don't."

Tina went to Amanda and Rachael's room. They, too, were without a phone. She went to Honey's and Ada's room, they didn't have a phone. Tina took a deep breath. She hated asking Jocelyn for anything, but with her luck, she figured there would be a phone in her room.

Tina knocked on Jocelyn's door. Jocelyn answered, "Hello."

"Jocelyn is there a phone in your room?"

As expected, Jocelyn answered, "Yes. You're welcome to use it?"

"Thanks."

"I need a couple of bottles of water," Jocelyn volunteered. "I'll go downstairs to get it. That way, you'll have some privacy."

"Thanks."

When Jocelyn returned to the room, Tina was just hanging up the phone. "Thanks again for the use of the phone."

"No problem." Jocelyn paused before continuing, "I really hate to bring this up, but I'm sure you'd want to know. Looking at the topographical map for tomorrow, we will be going over the worst countryside we have faced so far. If you walk tomorrow, I doubt you'll be in any shape to walk with the group the following day into Santiago. You must know how important it is for Faith to complete this pilgrimage with you and her daughter by her side. You should seriously consider resting tomorrow so you can keep up when we walk into Santiago."

Tina held her temper. "You may be right. I'll give it some thought."

Tina went down to the lobby and plopped down on a couch. She didn't want to delay Faith or the others on their last day into Santiago.

36

ARZUA TO O´ PINO

In the hotel lobby, when the seven gathered to begin their day, voices of guests were loud and chattering happily. Young people from all parts of the world socialized while they waited for more friends to join them.

Suddenly, Tina announced, "I'm not walking today. I'm going to take a cab to O´ Pino. I want to be well-rested so I can keep up tomorrow when we walk together into Santiago."

Amanda noticed her mother's look of shock.

Faith took a deep breath. "Tina, I'm sure today will be fine. Tomorrow we could simply get up earlier and start out before the others. That way we can walk with them into Santiago when they catch up."

"Faith, I'm going to hang out here for awhile. I'll meet you later this evening. Don't worry about me," Tina said sternly. "There's nothing you can say to change my mind."

Faith's annoyance turned to anger. The tone of her voice was harsh. "Tina, this is insane. You don't quit the day before we finish this pilgrimage. It doesn't make any sense."

"I'm not coming." Tina turned away.

Amanda went to her mother. "Mom, come on. You can't make her walk with us."

With a look of deep disappointment, Faith picked up her backpack to walk with Amanda and Rachael. The others had already started down the road. After walking less than a mile, Faith slowed down, directing her full attention to sending a message to Tina. Over and over again in her head, she yelled at Tina, "Tina this trail is easy. You can do this. It's an easy day. You can catch up to us. I'll go slow and wait for you."

"Amanda, you and Rachael go on. I'm going to wait here for Tina."

"Mom, what makes you think she's going to walk after that display this morning? She may have already taken a cab and gone to our hotel."

Her face worn with fatigue, Faith stared into space. "I've sent her a message. She'll come."

The distant look in her mother's eyes frightened Amanda. "Mom, are you okay?"

She waved her hands in front of her mother's face, trying to get her attention.

"Mom, please listen to us," Amanda pleaded.

Rachael stepped in front of Faith, saying anything she thought might pull her out of the trance. Faith still gave no signs of hearing what Rachael or her daughter said.

Unexpectedly, Amanda and Rachael heard what they thought was the sound of Tina's voice saying, "Stop yelling at me. I hear you. I'm almost there."

Faith eyes opened wide as a smiled formed.

Amanda looked up a trail where she saw Tina walking toward them with an unfamiliar male pilgrim.

"Where did you come from?" Amanda asked.

Tina took her male companion's hand. "This is Anthony. He's Italian and lives in Rome. I told him I needed to catch up to my friends. He knew of a short cut through the forest. I couldn't take Faith's continuous yelling at me. So, with Anthony's help, here I am."

"Tina, for a while Mom was in a daze. We couldn't get her to respond to anything."

By now, Faith's expression was pleasant and alert, as if nothing out of the ordinary had happened. Tina introduced Anthony to Faith. Faith greeted him, and gave him a big hug. "Thanks for helping my friend get back on the trail."

Anthony strolled along with them, sharing stories of his *Camino* adventures.

When Rachael and Amanda were a fair distance ahead of Faith and Tina, Rachael asked. "Has your mom ever done that before?"

"I haven't seen it happen before, but I've overheard comments she and her Shaman have spoken telepathically. Mom has mentioned experiencing a couple of out-of-body experiences. After listening to her recount some of these events, I bought her a book about it. I can't remember the title. It was something like, *How to Have an Out-Of-Body Experience in Ten Easy Lessons.* The book teaches how to use dreams to help with the process. I told her she could use the book as long as she didn't use it to visit me in my sleep. My heart couldn't take it."

"Well, it looks like she's mastered it. That was spooky, Tina coming along like that, saying she heard her calling."

"At least Tina's here, and Mom looks much happier."

The day passed quickly. Meeting and talking with other pilgrims added stimulation to the day's hike. They turned off the path to find their accommodations for the evening.

Faith looked at Amanda and Rachael, and said, "Tina and I are going to continue for awhile, and find somewhere ahead to stay the night. I figure that way, we'll have a head-start on you gals tomorrow. You'll catch up to us. Then, we can walk into Santiago together."

Amanda and Rachael were surprised, but not as surprised as Tina was. "You've got to be kidding! It will be dark soon. I'm tired, and it looks like it might rain."

"I'm not kidding. This is the only way. After tomorrow, you can sleep a week, but we need to get farther ahead tonight," Faith said.

"Can I at least stop and pee? And get something to eat and drink before we trudge off into the wilderness in the dark?" Tina asked in a very disgruntled tone.

"Of course, you can," Faith replied with a smile.

"Mom, are you sure you want to do this? We can walk slowly tomorrow," Amanda said.

"Slowly will not be an option. It's going to be exciting getting to Santiago. Believe me. I've thought about it a lot. I really think this is best. We're only a few hours from the next town."

"I can't believe how easily you say 'a few hours.' That's forever! But I'm too tired to argue with you at this point," Tina said.

After Faith and Tina ate and replenished their supplies, they left to hike the last portion of their day.

Within the hour, dusk was upon them, and daylight turned to a blue twilight. Soon a fine mist fell, making the ground mushy. The trail took them up a steep and slippery hill.

"We need to get to the next town before nightfall," Tina said.

The air filled with lingering wails, as lightning flashes illuminated the sky. As they trotted along, the path soon took them past an airport. "We must be getting close to civilization. That must be a town," Tina added, pointing to city lights.

They came to a crossroads where three routes were available to travel. After attempting two of the routes which brought them to barbed wire fences too high to climb over, they had to take the third route, which led deep into a dark cornfield. By the time they reached the end of the field, night was upon them. Tina looked up and down the deserted road. "There's nothing in sight. I don't see a single light anywhere. We are so very lost."

All of a sudden, headlights appeared as if out of a cloud of smoke. Tina rushed to the middle of the road waving her hiking poles to flag the car down. The car came to a screeching halt inches from her poles. Luckily, it was a cab.

The driver stuck his head out the window and introduced himself. "My name is Jesus." He smiled, and in perfect English, questioned. "What are two pretty girls like you doing alone out in the middle of nowhere so late at night?"

Before Tina could answer, Jesus pulled the cab to the side of the road, and got out of the car. From the light provided by his headlights, Faith noticed he was about her age, tall, and his appearance was pleasing to the eye.

He smiled, "Americans, yes? Crazy Americans, I think. Yes?"

"Yes," Faith replied. "We're on our way to Santiago. Do you know how far away we are from the city?"

"You're about five miles away. Would you like a ride to town?" he asked.

Faith answered quickly, "Oh no. We can't go there tonight. We need to walk in with our family and friends tomorrow."

Jesus gave them a strange look, "But you're going to Santiago? Yet, you don't want to go there?"

Faith smiled, "I know this sounds crazy." She told him where their hotel was and asked, "Can you take us there?" She paused, "And tomorrow, could you bring us back to a place close to here where we can get back on the *Camino*?"

"You could come to my home. You'd love my family. They'll make you dinner," Jesus offered.

"We'd love to, if it weren't already so late," Tina said reflecting sincere regret.

They all got into the cab. When they reached the hotel, Jesus helped them out of the cab, and while handing Faith her backpack, his mouth sloped into a gentle smile. Suddenly, Faith was in the arms of Jesus. He kissed her sweetly on the lips, "Until tomorrow."

Faith looked at Tina. "Don't say a word."

When they entered the lobby, they found the rest of the group sitting by the window at the hotel entrance.

Rachael was the first to speak. "So, who was that? And where have you two been?"

"It's not what it looks like. We got so lost we almost made it to Santiago. So don't worry, we'll be far enough ahead tomorrow you won't have to slow down for us," Faith said.

"We already ate. Mom, do you want me to get you a couple of sandwiches, and bring them to your room?"

"That would be great. After I get cleaned up, I won't feel like going out again, and I'm sure Tina would prefer to eat in as well.

"I think we're all calling it an early night," Amanda said.

That's the best news I've heard all day, Honey thought.

Earlier in the evening, Honey had made sure to ask for the room next to Amanda's and Rachael's room, using the excuse that her alarm clock was broken. She listened, and waited until well after 11:00 p.m. when the chatter in Amanda's room stopped. She waited another two hours to make sure those girls were asleep before she snuck into their room. Everything was going according to plan. She had taken the second key to their room and would leave it in their room after the deadly deed was complete. The thrill of completing the pilgrimage would be destroyed by Amanda's death, along with everything else Faith has ever believed in.

Honey climbed carefully out of bed. She placed pillows to look as if she were still in bed, in case Ada awoke and rolled over before her return. Honey inched her way to the door, turned the knob gently without making a sound. She took six small steps to Amanda's and Rachael's room, and cautiously opened their door. Both were sound asleep. Inch by inch, she gradually worked her way to Amanda's bedside. Moonlight flittered into the room through an open window when a vision of her sister, Margie appeared.

Honey saw her sister clearly, and heard Margie's voice plainly in her mind, *"Honey, don't do this! You don't need to do this. It won't help Ivan. He won't look out for you. He lies. Killing Amanda is wrong. Remember, we're good girls."*

Honey reached out to her sister and as she did Margie's body shifted into transparency and disappeared.

Amanda rolled over in bed. Honey gasped, but Amanda didn't wake. The moonlight glistened on Amanda's face.

Margie's vision reappeared and smiled at Honey sensing she would leave the room without doing harm.

Honey left the room, and switched the room keys back. Before returning to her room she tossed the syringe in a dumpster behind the hotel. Back in her room, she climbed into bed. She felt Margie's presence. In her mind, she spoke to her sister. *Faith may be guilty, but you are right. I can't kill Amanda. We are good girls.* Honey took in a deep breath. Tears formed in her eyes. For the first time on the trip she felt both a physical and emotional release, and prayed. *Dear God, forgive me and give me the courage to face Ivan and to convince him that forgiveness is the right thing to do.*

37

O´ PINA TO SANTIAGO DE COMPOSTELA

Smiles abounded as cameras clicked to document the final day of the pilgrimage.

"Rachael, can you move in a little closer to Tina?" Faith asked. "Amanda is still out of the picture."

A passerby seeing all the cameras being handed around, asked, "Would you like for me to take the picture so you can all get in the photo?"

"Thank you." Faith answered.

After photos were taken, Honey sat on a bench and thought. *She hoped Ivan would understand why she couldn't do it. But, whether or not he did she knew she had made the right decision. She had wasted so much of the trip. She didn't want to waste this day, too.*

"Honey, are you ready to go?" Ada asked.

Honey took a deep breath. "I know you girls were planning on walking in together and meeting up with

Faith and Tina down the road, but I'd rather walk alone for awhile and reflect on our journey."

Jocelyn said nothing and turned away. Ada nodded sympathetically. "I understand completely."

Amanda and Rachael held off telling Jocelyn they already had made plans to walk with a group they had met from Italy. Now, with Honey's announcement, Amanda felt even more uncomfortable in sharing their news. She braced and said, "We were thinking we would walk with some friends today, and catch up later in the day."

The stern look in Jocelyn's eyes directed toward Amanda and Rachael revealed total disgust. Ada gave the girls a friendly glance accompanied by a nod of understanding. Yet, her slow movement to pick up her backpack and limp posture relayed that she would miss their company. "See you gals in a few hours," Ada said as she picked up her backpack and left with Jocelyn.

An hour later, Faith and Tina's ride arrived at their hotel. Jesus stepped out of the cab, and with the warmest smile, greeted Faith. "Good morning, *Senorita.*" He took a step back, bowed, and held out a hand gesturing for Faith to enter the front passenger side of the cab. He opened the door and moved so close to Faith she could feel his breath on her neck. "Welcome, my beautiful lady." Jesus, noticed Faith's complexion glow a shade of pink, and he smiled as he turned away to put Tina's and Faith's backpacks and poles in the trunk of his cab.

After Faith was seated inside the cab and he had closed the door, he opened the back door for Tina, saying, "Please, *Senorita*, allow me." As soon as she was seated, he added, "I hope your morning has been a happy one so far. I found a spot where I can drop you ladies off near to where I found you last night."

Tina smiled, "Thanks."

At the end of a pleasant drive Faith received a lengthy hug and kiss good-bye.

When Jesus released her, he smiled and said, "Until we meet again. Maybe I will see you in Santiago."

Flushed, Faith nodded, thinking, *Oh, I hope not.*

"Hum. That was some good-bye. Are you going to tell Tom about your new boyfriend?" Tina smiled.

Faith laughed. "Are you going to tell Jimmy about your Italian boyfriend?"

Back on the path, Faith and Tina laughed about their previous night's adventure. "Tina, we must be behind the group that went to sunrise service, and in front of others making their way to Santiago today. There's not another soul in sight."

For the next hour, the two walked in silence. Faith immersed herself in thought. Everyday had been filled with uncertainties. They had lived on faith and depended on miracles. They had walked farther than anticipated, and often never knew if they were on the right path. Their patience was constantly worn thin from lack of sleep. They had forged along the tops of mountains, slid, slipped, and descended endless steps into valleys and hamlets to find refuge for the night, only to find they would have to hike up into the mountains again in the morning. They'd climbed over fallen trees, walked in rain and mud, pushed through forests, and grasses taller than the average woman. And the challenges never stopped.

Now all that stress has turned to joy. Faith embraced the days she awoke to the sounds of seagull cries, the aroma from bakery trucks and women calling to their children, the beauty of grass rippling over rolling hills by the power of the wind, and a small black-and-white dog persuading his flock of sheep to return to the safety of home.

How they laughed at butterflies as they danced silently around them while the sounds of birds, sheep, cows and their bells accompanied them on our walk. She hoped never to forget the sweet aromas of lavender and rosebuds as they climbed passed sheer cliffs of black rock, or the beautiful purple, blue, and white hydrangeas that graced winding country roads, and flowerbeds in front yards. She prayed that she'd never forget the mystical forests, surreal sunrises and sunsets, or the angels who appeared in the form of a farmer or villager pointing the way, offering water or a place to sit or rest when their feet wouldn't take them another step farther.

Faith and Tina came to the top of a hill. Tina looked to her left and saw a large compound. "This must be the last Alberge before Santiago. It looks like it covers a couple of miles. Can you imagine waking up here? Every pilgrim who has ever stayed here must have been thrilled to attend sunrise service before walking into Santiago. Want to wait here for the others?"

"Let's go a little farther. There's no place to sit here," Faith said.

A short distance down the road, they came to a small park where sculptures and other artifacts were on display. Tina laughed. "We must be getting close to Santiago. Look, there's a small building selling food and drink. They've got gourds hanging on the wall outside. I wanted to carry one with me. They're such a wonderful symbol of respect for past pilgrims who used them to carry water along the way. I couldn't find one this whole trip. Now, that we're almost there, I find one."

With an unhappy sigh, Faith said, "Well, I guess this means we are returning to civilization."

"Guess so," Tina added.

After sitting restlessly for an hour, Faith asked. "Want to walk a little farther?"

"Sure. It looks like it could still be a ways," Tina said.

A short distance down the path, they came to a ridge.

"The city looks as if it's still a long way from here." Tina said. "Maybe we should continue and wait closer to the city. It still might be some distance after we reach the city to get to the Cathedral. I don't want to hold the others up. Do you think Amanda and Rachael will be upset if we keep going?"

"Those girls will be happy to be with friends their age for as long as possible. I'm sure that won't be a problem long as we walk together into the city."

A little later, they came to the outskirts of Santiago. "We are so close. We better stop and wait here. If we go much farther, we'll be in the bustle of pilgrim activity, and it could be harder for us to find them, or vise versa," Faith said.

Two hours passed before they saw Jocelyn and Ada coming toward them. Faith and Tina rose to greet them. "We're almost there." Tina said.

"What are you doing waiting here? I hear the lines are long and unforgiving for *Camino* passport approval. Tina, since you've missed a few miles, the priests may not give you yours." Jocelyn said snidely.

"I'm sure she's covered enough miles to qualify." Faith said.

Jocelyn and Ada didn't respond, and continued on their way.

"Aren't you going to wait for Honey, Amanda, and Rachael?" Tina asked.

As Jocelyn and Ada walked away, Jocelyn answered. "No. I'm sure we'll see them at the Office of Peregrino. I don't feel like waiting all evening to get my *'Compostela'* issued."

Tina looked toward Faith. "Do you really think the priests will reject my *Camino* passport?"

"Of course not. You've walked almost the whole distance across Spain. They'd sign it if you only walked the last hundred kilometers. Stop worrying." Faith answered.

Amanda and Rachael arrived shortly after Jocelyn's and Ada's departure.

"Have you seen Honey?" Tina asked.

"Yep. She's not far behind. She seems to be taking her time. I think maybe she's savoring these last moments."

When Honey caught up to them, Faith felt like she was meeting her for the first time. *Amanda was right. There's something very different about her. She seems calmer, happier.*

In contrast to Faith's pleasant thoughts, Tina asked, "Have you ever seen so much horse poop?"

Caught off guard, Faith chuckled. "Since you've brought it up, the answer is, No! It's on the bridge and sidewalks. Everywhere. Horseback must be a popular way to travel the *Camino.*"

Together, Faith, Tina, Amanda, Rachael, and Honey walked the path to the edge of the city. They strolled through a well-maintained park admiring the historical monuments and statues honoring St. James, as well as other very notable pilgrims, such as Mother Teresa. All went well until they made a right turn and found themselves looking straight up a very steep, heavily-populated street. Tears formed in Tina's eyes when a friendly female passerby asked, "American? *Camino?*"

Tina nodded. To Tina's pleasure, the woman pointed down the hill. "The Cathedral is that way. It's in the heart of the city."

"*Gracias,*" Tina smiled and repeated, "*Gracias.*"

"Am I hearing things? Is that a bagpipe I hear?" Tina asked.

Suddenly, the sound of another bagpipe was heard by the group.

"It sounds like they're talking to each other from far away parts of the city. Bagpipes! Sounds funny to be listening to bagpipes in Spain! I feel like I should be in Ireland or Scotland," Rachael added.

The narrow and cobbled granite streets gave way to a time long since past. However, they did show signs of some modern accoutrements, and restaurants serving cappuccinos.

The buildings were nestled so close together that when they turned a corner, they were stunned to find they were in front of the Cathedral De Santiago. Taken by surprise, they stood silently mesmerized by its massive elegance and beauty.

"It's so big, and grand, and beautiful," Rachael said.

"Do you want to go in before we go to the Office of Peregrino?" Faith asked.

"I would," Honey answered.

"Me, too," Amanda and Rachael answered.

"Are you sure we have time?" Tina asked. "There could be a long wait."

"We should be fine. We have to go through or around the Cathedral to get to the office anyway, so let's go through quickly. We'll be back in the morning for Mass, but I assume the place will be a zoo then." Faith said.

"Okay, but let's not stay long. We can come back later after we get our passports signed," Tina said.

Inside, Rachael blurted out, "Wow, wow, and triple wow. Look, there's the column and the pilgrim's hand-print. I read that pilgrims have been placing their hands inside the print for centuries." When Rachael stepped toward the column, a man dropped to his knees beside it. His hands were folded in prayer. Before taking turns placing their hands in the imprint Rachael and the others waited until the man had finished his prayer, placed his hand in the handprint, and left. Faith noticed Tina's eyes were tearing. Rachael and Amanda each approached in silence. Faith was well aware that her eyes were watering as well when she placed her hand in the imprint.

"Mom, look, there's the statue of St. James. Pilgrims are going up those steps to hug the statue as a way of giving thanks for their safe passage. There isn't a very long line. Tomorrow after Mass, I bet it will be really crowded. We should go now," Amanda suggested.

"I hate to admit it, but she's probably right," Tina said.

The staircase leading to the statue was short, steep, and narrow. Each pilgrim who reached the platform behind the statue paused, reached out, and then hugged the statue.

Faith watched as each person took their turn. *Something amazing, even miraculous is happening.* When she hugged the statue of St. James, she recalled once more the day she asked God to allow a statue to wink at her. He hadn't obliged. She smiled then thanked God for all the miracles He had sent her all her life.

Before leaving, they visited the Cathedral's catacombs to see the crypt of St. James. Then, with reverence, they exited the Cathedral and entered the main square. They crossed the square, and without another delay, went straight to the Office of Peregrino.

The lines were short. Each pilgrim faced an assigned priest or official reviewer who examined the *Camino* passports and issued the official declaration, the '*Compostela.*'

Faith presented her *Camino* Passport to the priest and answered his question. "Why did you walk the path of St. James?

"To help a friend." Before leaving, she turned to the priest, "And to find my way back to God."

When the priest handed Faith her Passport, she felt like an angel in flight. She looked down the counter where Amanda, Rachael and Honey had already received their *Composetella's.* Faces beaming with pride, they held them in the air. Faith nodded in approval and held hers up, too.

Faith looked at Tina who was still talking to the priest. She noticed the strained look on Tina's face. Suddenly, Tina's look of concern changed to delight. She turned and moved away from the counter, holding her *Compostella* close to her heart, and with tears of joy, she smiled contently.

In joyful silence, they wandered in unison back to the Cathedral's square. There, they found places to sit on stone walls and watched other pilgrims arrive.

While Faith watched pilgrims arrive, sadness overcame her. She didn't want the pilgrimage to end. She took solace in the fact that they still had four more days before their travels would end. They still had to get to the *(Cape Finisterre) The End of the World*.

Monastery of San Martin Pinario

38

SANTIAGO DE COMPOSTELA

Following a night of delightful celebration out on the town, clean and dressed in their best clothes saved for this day, the group met for breakfast before Mass. After breakfast, together the seven walked the narrow streets to the Cathedral, and stopped in front of the Monastery of San Martin Pinario.

Rachael pulled out her guide book and read, "It was built in 1494, and founded by Italian Benediction monks to watch over the remains of St. James. Little remains of the original medieval monastery. A small portion houses a seminary and school of theology."

They arrived an hour before Mass was to begin, only to find the Cathedral was already packed. Locating a pew where they could sit together was a challenge, but true to form Rachael accomplished the deed.

While Faith took note of the church's magnificent grandeur, her eyes stopped to observe a procession of nuns taking their places near the altar. Minutes later, their song emanated through the Cathedral sending chills down to Faith's spine: *Every soul must be filled with God's love listening to these majestic songs sung a cappella.*

Faith had read that there were usually 25 concelebrant priests assisting the Cardinal who celebrated the Mass. During Mass, when the priests' voices filled the Cathedral, she was amazed how the strength of their male vocals could be even more inspiring than that of the nuns. She had also read about the *Botafumerio*, the largest incense burner. But when she saw it being carried down the center aisle, she knew she'd never be able to describe the experience adequately. Eight red-robed *tirableiros* attached the *Botafumeiro* to the pulley mechanism which began to swing like a giant pendulum.

Rachael leaned toward Amanda and Faith and whispered as she expounded while reading through the guidebook. "Over the years there have been a number of accidents that occurred during the swinging of the *Botafumeiro*. Luckily, none recently. In past years, the *Botafumeiro* was attached to the rope with a ceiling hook which sometimes became disconnected. It's secured by "sailor knots" now. One of the most renowned accidents took place during a visit by Princess Catherine of Aragon. She was on a journey to marry the heir to the British throne in 1499 and stopped by the Cathedral De Santiago. While it was being swung, the *Botafumeiro* flew out of the Cathedral through the Platerias high window. No one was injured."

As the *Botafumeiro* swung through the Cathedral, Faith watched in amazement while Rachael continued reading. "It weighs 80 kilograms and will reach speeds up 60 kilometers an hour. That's about 176 pounds traveling at almost 38 miles per hour. It's the largest incense burner in the world and is made of brass and bronze and silver plated. They say its original purpose was to mask the stench from hundreds of unwashed pilgrims."

As the *Botafumeiro* swung higher and higher over the heads of the congregation, Faith thought, If one monk sneezes, the huge urn will fall and hundreds could be injured. It swung harder and farther, over more and more parishioners, then abruptly, the priests slowed the *Botafumeiro's* arc until it came to a stop. Silent reverence for the Mass was lost the minute the urn stopped. Everyone in the Cathedral applauded.

Faith mentally left behind the trials of the trip as a profound peace and natural tranquility captured her mind and body.

While in this dream-like-state, she listened to the Cardinal announce the names of the pilgrim groups in attendance. Countries from all over the world were represented including China, Germany, Japan, France, Austria, England, and everywhere else. When they announced their group from the United States, Faith could have sworn the statue of St. James winked at her. She looked at her group and thought. *We have reached our Mecca, and the legend continues.*

39

CAPE FINISTERRE (THE END OF THE WORLD)

This morning would be the last day the seven would see each other before going their separate ways. Flights for Jocelyn, Ada, and Honey had been scheduled for them to leave Spain two days after arriving in Santiago. The rest of the group was to depart for The End of the World (Cape Finisterre) the same day the others would fly home.

At breakfast, Faith initially was saddened by the lack of conversation between them. But by the time her cappuccino arrived she hand a change of heart, thinking, *This pilgrimage turned out just the way it was supposed to. Tina is ready to go home with love replacing anger and she is in such better shape physically. New horizons have opened up for Amanda and Rachael. Amanda and I have had this experience together to cherish forever. I believe in miracles, and today I will travel to the End of the World with my daughter, my best friend, and my very own special tour guide, Rachael. I should feel ecstatic, but I don't. I'm going to miss being a pilgrim.*

In the midst of this silence, Rachael blurted out, "I can't wait to burn these clothes."

"You do realize before you get to burn those clothes, we still have another four days of hiking in front of us," Tina said jovially.

"I almost wish I had decided to go on with you gals," Ada said, "I did say 'almost'."

After breakfast, lighthearted good-byes were followed by hugs and well wishes. No matter what issues still lingered, Faith could see looks of sadness in each person's eyes accompanying the marking of the end of a triumphal pilgrimage.

Faith, Tina, Amanda, and Rachael put on their packs, and waved their last good-byes to the others.

"Mom, look. There's that Spanish couple."

Faith called out, "Maria."

Maria waved and she and her husband stopped to wait for them.

"Did you bring your clothes to burn?" Rachael asked.

Maria smiled, "Not all, but a few pieces. More symbolic than necessary."

"Us too," Amanda said.

Smiles abounded along with pleasant conversation as they began their trek to Negreira.

After two hours of hiking through beautiful countryside, they came to a small village. Rachael noticed a tapas bar. "Would anyone else like to stop for something to eat?"

All expressed a need to take a break.

While orders were taken, Faith whispered to Tina, "Tina, you are doing fabulously today. You're keeping up with the entire group."

"I guess a few days rest, plus a well-maintained trail helps, but I know Maria and John will probably pick up their pace as the day progresses. And when they do, I'll be just fine. Honestly, I couldn't be happier."

Four hours into the day, Amanda's, Rachael's, John's, and Maria's pace did not pick up. Yet, to Tina's surprise, they caught up to another group walking even slower. That group was from England on holiday with a tour group. Their trip started in Santiago and they were to walk to Cape Finisterre. One of the women told Tina that they were staying at the same hotel.

Six hours from the start of the day, only half an hour behind Rachael and Amanda, Faith and Tina arrived at the country house of Coton.

Amanda and Rachael sat in the lobby when Faith, Tina, and a few women from the tour entered the country house. Tina introduced her new friends to Amanda and Rachael. "This is, Carolyn and Jill. They're from London, England."

"We've met others from your group. It sounds like we'll probably see you later at dinner," Amanda said.

"Did you stop at the chapel dedicated to St. Maurus?" Rachael asked.

"We did," Tina answered, "It reminded me a little of a small chapel I went to in upstate New York built by Tiffany. The stained glass windows were beautiful."

When Carolyn and Jill were out of ear range, Tina said, "I love their accents, don't you?"

"I do," Faith answered.

Laughter was the menu of choice at dinner.

When morning came, Tina was up and ready to go.

Carolyn and Jill, along with a few members of their group were already at the breakfast table when Amanda, Rachael, Tina and Faith arrived.

The day began with their passing the Barcala river, and continued along the mountainside where they climbed the hillside of Monte Aro. At the four hour mark, they stopped for lunch at a spot where they viewed the Ferenza dam.

"This day is going to be a long one," Carolyn said.

"You both look to be in great shape," Faith said. "Are you Munro baggers? I hear this type of hiking in Scotland is becoming the new rage."

"We are. Not many Americans are familiar with Munro bagging. We're both teacher's. And we try to go on one adventure each summer. Our husbands prefer cycling trips, but they do join us for hikes as well," Carolyn answered.

"How about you? I am very impressed that you have walked the entire *Camino*. I would like to do it someday," Jill said.

When Tina heard they would have another four to five hours before getting to their bed-and-breakfast, she thanked God that she had six weeks to prepare for these few days.

Seeing the look of concern of Tina's face at the announcement of such a long day, Faith quietly reminded her that she had covered countryside much tougher for upwards of 12 hours and survived. "Besides," Faith said, "tomorrow will be a beautiful coastal walk along cliffs and by coves. The day's walk is estimated at only four to five hours."

"I love your *only* four to five hours."

Faith smiled.

The day ended with the sea rising to meet them. Fatigue drifted away, replaced by the joy of dinner with friends and family.

The following morning, Faith had that same dreadful feeling she had the day before walking into Santiago. *We're almost there. This is it. One more day then I will no longer be a pilgrim.*

Faith assumed Amanda, Rachael, and Tina were feeling something similar because they hung around after breakfast waiting for the others to get a head-start so they could walk together.

"This reminds me of our first days walking along the sea," Amanda said.

Rachael and Tina's eyes watered as Faith nodded in agreement.

"Tomorrow's it. We'll be at The End of the World. Then it's back to Santiago. I'm going to miss this life," Rachael said.

"Believe it or not, so will I," Tina said.

Together they walked to the sea. Cresting a hill, the sea in front of them took on a haunting persona.

"No wonder mariners of past years thought this was 'The End of the World,'" Tina said.

"Well, are we going to burn our clothes like the pilgrims of the past, and walk bare-assed on the path to the sea?" Rachael asked jokingly.

"Not me. But I'll be happy to burn what I brought with me first chance we get," Faith answered.

They soon found a spot where others clothes had been burned. Faith, Tina, Amanda, and Rachael threw the clothes they'd brought into the pit, lit their clothes, and watched them burn. As the last embers died, Faith pulled out a bottle of champagne and four paper cups. She poured champagne for each, and held her glass in the air. "To a job well done."

After their toast, they took their drinks by the shore to sit and watch the sunset. Faith felt she had never seen a sunset so beautiful. She looked down the beach and saw the silhouette of two people cuddling as they watched the sun go down. She had seen their silhouette before. She tapped Tina on the shoulder and whispered, "There are our Spanish friends."

Faith held back the words she wanted to say, *I hope to enjoy an adventure like this with Tom someday,* knowing for Tina walking with Jimmy would never be a reality.

She felt as if she was saying good-bye to Spain forever. Tomorrow they would start the day with a two hour walk in the morning. This would be followed by a 45 minute bus ride to Santiago. She didn't want to think about how tough that bus ride was going to be.

Fireworks of Cathedral de Santiago

40

RETURN TO SANTIAGO

For two hours hearts fluttered and feet moved slowly as Faith's group and other tourists crossed through the beautiful countryside to catch the bus to Santiago.

On the bus, laughter remained hearty while pilgrims shared highlights of their trip. Yet, in between the words, in the silence, sadness lingered denoting the end of the journey.

The bus arrived in Santiago at 1:00 p.m. finding the stores were still open, Faith, Tina, Amanda, and Rachael decided to get manicures and pedicures before taking siestas.

Following a delightful afternoon on the way back to their hotel, Rachael excitedly announced, "We'll need the rest this afternoon. After all, we will be up all night celebrating the Festival of St. James. Nights in Spain are always alive with parties, but today the excitement seems a hundred times greater. I can't imagine what the festivities will be like this evening."

"I know you're right about that," Tina said. "I've got a feeling we won't sleep at all this evening. I sure wish my family was here."

"I know what you mean. Tom would have loved this. If I had known how fabulous this was going to be I would have insisted he come to Spain in time for the festival."

Faith looked up and gazed across the street. She couldn't believe her eyes. Tina's daughter and son stood by Tom's side as he pushed Jimmy's wheelchair toward them.

When Tina saw Jimmy, the delight in her eyes could have opened the gates to heaven. Tina ran to meet her family.

Tom, cool as ever, went to Faith and Amanda. He kissed Amanda on the forehead, and then took Faith in his arms and kissed her tenderly on the lips. Faith thought. *No kiss has ever been so sweet.*

Tom said, "I've booked two extra rooms, one for Tina's kids, and another for you and me." Faith smiled.

At the hotel, after getting settled in their rooms the group met in the hotel restaurant. For the next two hours, everyone shared their last seven weeks of escapades. Then, it was time for siesta. Faith's and Tom's siesta was delayed while they got reacquainted in bed. Faith hadn't realized just how much she had missed her lover. An hour later, with a satisfied smile on her face, Faith curled up in Tom's arms. She slept, and for the first time since the trip began, slept peacefully.

When Faith awoke, she gave Tom a warm hug. "We're all planning an early dinner at 8:00 p.m."

Tom laughed, "8:00 p.m.? Early?"

"In Spain, do as the Spaniards do. We figure, to insure getting a spot where we can watch the fireworks without Jimmy's wheelchair getting in someone's way, we better try and get to the square as soon as possible."

After a celebratory dinner, Tina pushed Jimmy's wheelchair over cobblestone roads. When the walkway turned upward, Tom quickly took over the pushing and steering for Tina. "Thanks, Tom," Tina said.

While they strolled amongst hundreds of people from around the world, they enjoyed being entertained by young teens.

"Don't you love the colorful, traditional costumes the kids are wearing?" Amanda asked.

"My favorite is the group from Norway. I love their hats and the beautiful embroidery on their clothes," Rachael said.

"Did you notice that these young groups sing and dance to their traditional music, but have incorporated a popular beat into it? They've modernized traditional sounds. I love it," Amanda said.

"I thought there was something unique about the music. I especially loved the music the Portuguese group shared. I think I'll go back and buy one of their CDs. I understand that sales from the CDs help to pay the kids expenses," Tom said.

In the square, they found a spot off to the side with a great view of the Cathedral. It was already 10:00 p.m. when they arrived, the time the fireworks were scheduled to begin.

"I was sure the place would already be too full for us to get a spot," Faith said.

"Mom, haven't you figured out Spanish time yet? It's still early for this group."

Faith smiled, "When you're right, you're right."

They got comfortable. Over the next half hour the square filled to capacity. A procession began at 10:30 p.m. on a walkway behind them that led to a balcony on the Administration Building across the square from the Cathedral. Famous artists, musicians, movie stars, high-ranking priests, Cardinals, and politicians worked their way up to the balcony. Over the next hour people in the square cheered as celebrities continued to make their grand entrances. Then, the King and Queen of Spain stepped out onto the balcony. Over loudspeakers, the voices of nuns singing a cappella from within the cathedral could be heard, and people in the square went crazy cheering and applauding.

Emotions were electric. Organ music introduced a brilliant light show. For an hour, scenes of nature, unusual characters, and mystical creatures formed by colorful lights moved across the Cathedral's outer walls. Suddenly, the music hit a crescendo. Everyone knew something amazing was about to occur. From every window and doorway of the Cathedral, fireworks burst out in every direction.

"I've never seen so many shapes and colors of fireworks before," Tina said.

Jimmy took Tina's hand. "This is amazing. It looks as if the entire Cathedral is on fire. I wonder how the interior is being protected. There must be hundreds of fireworks all being fired at the same time." Jimmy took a moment before continuing. "You know this was Tom's idea to come and join you. I'm so glad he got us here."

For the next three hours they cheered, laughed, and remained mesmerized by the splendor of the music and the unbelievable fireworks.

Holding Tom's hand, Faith looked at the delighted faces of her friends and daughter. *It doesn't get any better than this.*

41

THE FINAL REPORT
1992 – DOWNSTATE CORRECTIONAL
FACILITY, FISHKILL, N.Y.

Slowly, forebodingly, Honey entered the prison corridor. The gleam in her eyes and the robust swing in her step were no longer present. Her head hung low as she entered the visitors' room to face her love. Even after spending time traveling with Faith and Amanda, Honey still believed in Ivan's innocence. She prayed he would forgive her for not killing Amanda. He had to. She loved him.

E P I L O G

In 2006 when I walked the *Camino Del Norte* I had no idea that I would transform the experience into a fictional tale. After all, the characters for my first novel *The Final Act* had not even entered my mind. And even after these characters developed, I had no idea that I would later set them off on a pilgrimage.

Still, after I finished this story, I felt compelled to share a few details from my real-life experience.

Six other women and I walked the *Camino*, each at our own pace. All of us were at least twenty years older than the oldest character in my book, all over the age of 50. I did not have the pleasure of traveling with any family member, and we never encountered a character even closely related to Honey. The paths, places we stayed, and people we met along the way were relayed as close to true as I remember.

In the tale *Crossroads,* the character Tina faced the same challenges as the rest, but she faced them with added hardships. One of the women on our trip faced the *Camino* with physical challenges that put more demands on her than anything my character Tina had to face. She was an inspiration to many on the path and still is to me. I mention this because so many friends after hearing that I walked the *Camino* told me that they would love to travel the *Camino* someday. Then, they would add reasons why they couldn't. Usually at that point, they mention some sort of aliment that would impede them.

What I usually discover at a later date, is their real concern is fear they may not be able to complete the journey.

There have been times when I have taken on challenges and failed miserably. I may be different than some, but probably not so much. The fact is that my personal growth as a human being has come as much, if not more, from my failures as my successes.

One day, while walking the *Camino*, I thought, *What if the idea of reincarnation is true, and we are coming back.*

If I don't face my fears this time, I'll only have to face them the next time, or the time after that.

What if the atheists are right and we're just going to die and overtime our molecules will disburse over the universe?

Then, I will have missed out on the experience and never will the opportunity present itself again.

What if like in so many religions, if I live a good life, I make it to heaven?

But by not facing my fears now, will I miss all that heaven has to offer?

THE END

25805997R00171

Made in the USA
Charleston, SC
15 January 2014